Make Way for Baby!

A Collection of Judeo-Christian Poetry

M. LEANNE TODD

WESTBOW
PRESS®
A DIVISION OF THOMAS NELSON
& ZONDERVAN

WestBow Press books may be ordered through booksellers or by contacting:

WestBow Press
A Division of Thomas Nelson & Zondervan
1663 Liberty Drive
Bloomington, IN 47403
www.westbowpress.com
1 (866) 928-1240

ISBN: 978-1-5127-6887-9 (sc)
ISBN: 978-1-5127-7331-6 (e)

Print information available on the last page.

WestBow Press rev. date: 3/3/2017

Contents

Foreword - My Testimony

If anyone comes speaking in the name of the LORD Jesus Christ, it is imperative that their lives become an open book. That is because having intimate knowledge of the author's life allows people to have a better perspective and sense of discernment about what is written. For this reason, I feel it necessary to share not only about the strength of my faith with the reader of this collection, but also...about my *weakness*.

I was diagnosed with bipolar disorder at a young age in life – my 9th grade year in high school. One day I began to physically shake in my gym class. I don't remember that. I only remember being escorted to the school office, where the general consensus was that I had been "doing drugs." There I suffered a brief interrogation about my would-be drug connections, for which I had no coherent answers.

I sat, bracing for the impending wrath of a militant anti-drug regime and whatever authorities would be called...you know, for BACK UP, against this wily and decidedly *baked* honor roll student. Fortunately, only my mother was called. She could be plenty frightening in her own rite, but at least she didn't carry a gun—usually. (You must realize, this all happened in Texas. And Texas is a state where signs forbidding firearms must be posted on the doorsteps of convalescent homes.)

Eventually I was taken to the local emergency room, and from there I was ultimately sent to the DePaul Center in Waco, Texas. I would spend the next few months in that private hospital which focused on treating various conditions in adolescents such as: substance abuse, mental illnesses, eating disorders, and so forth.

Despite one doctor's firm prognosis of bipolar disorder, otherwise known as manic-depression, the staff ran with an initial diagnosis of schizophrenia. Lithium, the most effective drug used for bipolar disorder in the 1980's, had certain dangerous side effects that other drugs did not have. So, to ere on the side of caution, the hospital's medical majority ruled and they began to treat me with drugs that were typically used for schizophrenia.

That is when my ordeal only became worse. I have vague memories of ambling around in circles and squares with my arms mounted at my sides like some robot. I have other foggy memories of angry faces demanding that I take a shower. But I didn't know how to make the water warm; it was always cold. And *it hurt* to be in the cold water.

I was alone. There was nothing familiar in that place. Sterile, generic furniture—the same in every room. Strange faces, strange voices. I would crawl through a maze of confusion and anxious feelings all day, every day—unaware of space and time, stumbling around in concentric circles or rigid squares like some lab rat unable to find an exit to the winding hallways...or from my existence.

I remained in that disoriented state for some time until the DePaul Center was about to have me transported to a state hospital. But just before my scheduled transfer, the hospital staff finally acquiesced to the first doctor's insistence that they treat me with medications for bipolar disorder. Nothing else had worked, so they had no room to argue with him.

And voila—within ten days of being on that medication, I could, at least, *function* to some degree. I could shower myself and speak coherent sentences. A few more days later, and my old personality had mostly returned with the use of Lithium, a chemical *salt* on the periodic chart of elements.

But treatment with Lithium had to be monitored closely in the initial trial. This required frequent blood tests to determine how much of the medication was in my bloodstream. The doctors had to make sure that this medication was at a therapeutic, but not *toxic* level.

Every morning from that point on, I would rouse to the jarring clicks of the door handle to my little room being opened. The dim light from the hallway, eclipsed by the nurse's figure, would soon spill onto my face as I laying squinting upward in effort to discern which staff member was on duty this time. I would then wake fully to the sound of rubber gloves snapping into position, and unknown fingers pressing into my arm to find a vein. I remember the shiny sight of their supply kits, which was about as comforting as the metal tray of tools that dentists must lay out before you. The instruments were a subtle reminder of who is going to be in charge for the next few minutes. Then would come their gentle preparation with the words, "This is going to stick a little." And in would go the needle, a tiny rod held firmly in soft tissue until the blood was drained. Then would come the cumbersome jolt as the nurse would replace the full vial with an empty one; sometimes a total of three vials were taken at one drawing. Upon discharge, my arms were blackened and bruised beyond belief. My veins had been torn so much that blood had spilled into my skin creating dark purple and blue blotches several inches above and below each elbow. But no matter—the word "discharge" was all I needed to hear.

Or so I thought.

One last level, and no more to come for six months. Hallelujah. Since it was now "slim pickins" among the veins in my arms...the discharge nurse determined that taking blood from my hand was the only viable option.

So first came the cold, sterile stench of rubbing alcohol and the dreadful angst in my stomach as packages were being opened in a hurried rustle. Of course the experience would not be complete without the sinister glint of fluorescent lighting that flickered off the newly exposed needle tip. This would be a way of life from now on, like diabetes, they said—no point in complaining.

As I watched the tiny spearhead of the needle pierce the top of my young hand, it was in that moment of faint Christ-like imagery that God spoke...not in words so much as in gentle notions. He imparted to me,

"Many have come before you, among them, your Elder Brother, Who is much bigger and stronger than you will *ever* have to be. He endured far worse. And He is *here*—in this tiny, small town lab room."

I was just a child, around 14 years old. All that really interested me was eating my fill of brownies and listening to Madonna. I was just one of a million other misfit Raggedy Anne and Andies who frequented that rehab unit, and a small and seemingly insignificant one at that. So these notions seemed extraneous, illogical. And yet in that moment when my young blood spurted full into the vial, more notions came to comfort me,

"You are Mine now, more than ever. You belong to Me. You are safe with your Brother, here for My purpose, and I will always be with you."

But what purpose could come from such a broken life?

I had been saved by Christ right before my parent's divorce the previous year after reading His Gospels, but still had very little knowledge of the Bible, and could only count on one hand the number of times that I'd been inside a church as a small child.

So how could I, in my ignorance and eccentricities, be of worth or of use to anyone—much less to YAHWEH...the Supreme Being of the universe?

I did not entertain those questions. They were good ones, but simply not strong enough to penetrate the warmth and joy I felt from this new sense of divine inclusion. Rich, red blood had filled the vial. The sample was complete. I flinched at the exiting needle, and smiled with my LORD. Little did I know...that such lives, are His specialty.

You see, in decades to come...I would suffer three more manic episodes that would, again, require hospitalization each time. And even to this day, I must manage this illness with medications through proper psychiatric care. Just as the Apostle Paul would always have the thorn in his flesh; this illness, it would not go away. But what I have found in Scripture, is that the Apostle was actually *blessed* to have his thorn. Clearly, the Christ told Paul, "...My grace is sufficient for you, for My strength is made perfect in weakness." (2nd Corinthians 12:9 NKJV)

When we are stripped, and broken, laid bare by this world and its fallen state as manifested in our own human weakness and frailty...the less when can rely upon our*selves*. And the more we must cling to His grace, the closer to Him we become. I believe this is what led Paul to further proclaim in 2nd Corinthians 12:9-10 (NKJV), "Therefore most gladly I will rather boast in my infirmities, that the power of Christ may rest upon me. Therefore I take pleasure in infirmities, in reproaches, in needs, in persecutions, in distresses, for Christ's sake. For when I am weak, then I am strong."

Since that first manic episode, I have married and given birth to three wonderful children, one of whom has severe Autism, Intellectual Disabilities, and Diabetes. Through it all my husband and I have been married for over 24 years. I am an active member in my local church and by God's grace I am able to contribute to our community. I live a productive and well-adjusted life. But how is this all of this even possible after all that I have been through?

Clearly, the medications I take are *necessary* to ensure the stability of my moods, rest, and even sanity. I won't argue that.

However, they are NOT what (or *Who*) has...quite literally...*restored my soul.*

Truly, a person can be completely "sane" and simultaneously *miserable* – defeated, humiliated, and disgraced. But by the grace of God, I am none of those things anymore. Everyday, I have my challenges and my struggles as we all do...but there is a hope in me; there is JOY; there is life. And these attributes are not my own.

I know this because of times when I have drifted from the LORD, over the course of my life thus far...and I know the painful consequences of falling into that separation: angst, worry, arrogance, hatred for my fellow man over the slightest infraction, impatience, greed, covetousness, and the list of sins go on and on.

But when I take in the Gospel, and know that all these sins which separate me from the Holy God have been crucified with Christ in His perfect sacrifice for us on the cross...a joy feels me, a relief, a new found freedom stirs in me with the knowledge that nothing I can do or have done is of merit; that I don't have to "earn" my own salvation, that rather – it was *given* to me as a precious gift.

As it is written in John 3:16 (NKJV), "For God so loved the world, that He gave His only begotten Son, that whoever believes in Him shall not perish but have everlasting life."

It is then that I know where to credit this peace that surpasses all understanding! It is not derived from a trial-free life of ease and comfort. Nor is it to be credited to the local drug store, that much is for sure—and certainly not to my*self.*

But when I bow <u>in daily repentance,</u> in turning from my sins, to the Omnipotent, Almighty God...YAHWEH, the Ancient of Days...through CHRIST, He lifts me from my knees so that I can mount up on the wings of eagles. (Isaiah 40:31 NKJV) He restores my soul. (Psalm 23:3 ESV)

When my heart threatens to fail...He becomes the strength of my heart and my portion forever. (Psalm 73:26 NIV) And most importantly, I am reborn! (John 3:1-8 KJV)

This is because unyielding truth and amazing grace have been embodied together in a Living Man, Who is the Living GOD. His name is YESHUA, Jesus Christ. And only *He*...can set you *free*. (John 8:31-36 NASB)

Make Way for Baby! *Isaiah 40:3 NIV, John 1:23 ESV

He's been waiting patiently
for many months so long.
He's been nesting nice and cozy
in His womb and growing strong.

And now He has decided
to come tearing out--
through cramping muscles,
burning flesh,
and spines that splinter into!
He'll leave us shaking, trembling
'fore His glorious task is through!

But I wonder if He'll be upset…
or angry at a few
of His well-intentioned relatives
for whom
He's overdue.

For some haven't been prepared
to make an offering,
to welcome Him into this world
for all His suffering.

Some haven't been excited
about His soon arrival…
instead we've wondered if
He'll inconvenience our survival.

"Will this Baby hurt us…?
Will He demand too much…?
Time and money spent
toward all His needs and such…?"

"Will Baby make us miserable
living on the
straight and narrow...?"
Well, misery does love company
with every fallen sparrow--

into crime and rape and vicious lies
that lead us to the hearse.
I think it's safe to say,
without Him,
we've done worse.

I bet we'll be relieved
to see what joy
Baby brings...
see Him forgive
our sins,
our stains,
and all our shortcomings.

We'll see Him comfort and love us   *Romans 5:8 NIV
despite the way we are...
if we repent
He'll wipe our eyes   *Revelation 21:4 NKJV
from wrongs made near and far.

And now at last – He's coming!
I feel my sides seize up!
But for all my crippling pain
I cannot drink from this, His cup.   *Matthew 26:39 ESV

Can't others feel this pressure
in all surrounding areas?
Surely, I'm not the only
sainted mother*   *Galatians 4:19 NLT
in hysteria.

So soon, sweet rapture,
we'll see His face--
all else will melt behind Him.
All fear and doubt and agonies,
His touch
will bless and bind them.

This Baby offers love,   *John 3:16 NKJV
it's what He comes to share...
along with peace eternally--   *John 14:27 NASB
if our own cross, we bear.   *Matthew 16:24 ESV

Author's Note:
In writing this poem years ago, I was moved by two things:
the "rebirth" of the human soul;
and the return of Christ to this world.

Right now, perhaps more than ever, this world seems to be in the beginning of sorrows, birth pangs...something that I, as a mother, am well familiar with. This world is gripped – torn between its selfish wants and the "Child" that came so long ago and Who will come again.

The world labors...fearing the demands this Child will bring, just as young first time parents always do a little, no matter how much the child is wanted. The pastor who introduced me to the Christ decades ago would always say that before salvation we all have this sense of "LORD... not yet. Let me have my life for a little while longer." But we all have to come to terms with His decree, that he who keeps his life will loose it... eternally.

And truly, the kind of love we humans know is not all that will be expected of Christians in any age. We can "love" our dog or that perfect cup of coffee. Human love can be very self-serving and conditional, subject to change when we have been wronged or when we are simply distracted. But when Christ saves us, it is not our own love that we will be compelled to share, but His. And His love is deep, vast, and wide: deep enough to quench all thirsts, ease all pains, and lift all spirits; vast enough to span the universe and wide enough to span the cross. As such, His love will not allow us to ignore the lost and suffering. His love will sustain us to carry a *cross*. He will ignite a holy, consuming fire in us – and with it, we will light the nations.

A Prayer for Revival

I know You from the days of old,   *Hebrews 13:8 NIV
I know Your strength and Spirit, bold!

I know You though my struggles are
deep and high and wide and far.

I know that you have rescued me
with all your love on Calvary's Tree!   *Luke 23:33, John 19:17 - NKJV

But all I know is limited,   *1 Corinthians 13:12 NLT
for You, oh LORD, are from some hid...   *Matthew 13:13,Luke
10:24 - NASB

Your mysteries are yet unveiled
to children, meek, who've not withheld...   *Mark 10:15 ESV

their pride and ego - sweet life itself   *Matthew 16:25, Luke 9:24 - NIV
praise and prayers, time and wealth -

yet through a clouded mirror see   *1 Corinthians 13:12 NLT
we all your glory, truth and He...

Who gave His life and died for us,   *Romans 5:8 NKJV
for Whom we pine and witness much   *Acts 1:8 NASB

Oh, let us see Him face to face -   *Genesis 32:30 NIV
let sin not be our resting place!

But make us rise as old dry bones   *Ezekiel 37:1-14 KJV
did in the valley from Your throne!

Ezekiel did prophesy,
and now I call on You, Most High!

Rain down your love and flood this earth,   *Hosea 6:1-3 NASB
awaken us in great rebirth!   *Ephesians 5:14 NKJV

Hide not Your face that shelters all,   *Psalm 27:9 NIV
but quench the thirst of righteous call...   *Matthew 5:6 ESV

with Your sweet water, living pure -   *John 4:14 NLT
and let our sickened hearts endure...   *Jeremiah 17:9 NASB

all shame for you and for your cross,
but let us bring Him to the lost!

Open their eyes, let their ears hear
that You are mighty, gracious, NEAR!   *Psalm 34:18 ESV

For them, I love, and them I pray—
let Your Strong Spirit lead the Way...   *John 14:6 NKJV

that leads, though narrow, straight to life   *Matthew 7:14 NIV
and brings great joy among the strife!   *John 15:11 ESV

I know You from the days of old,
I'll know You til my blood runs cold...

for Your great grace and Kingdom's sake -
arise Your bride, may she *awake!* *Ephesians 5:32, Romans 13:11 - NKJV

A Very Important Date

Running so late for her wedding
in the streets and surely heading...

down any old cold dark alley
and back-sliding in the valley,

seeking detours that can't be found
taking direction so unsound.

Unprepared
    for this coming Day
the bride
    has lost sight of her Way.   *John 14:6 NIV

So she waits and pines instead
by the graves, among the dead...

longing for some sweet release
she finds no joy,
    strength,
        or peace.

She hungers for her wedding feast,
but lies
    as bait for the stray beast...

who roams all about to devour   *1 Peter 5:8 NKJV
the bride and maids until the hour—

will come
    to take them
        off the streets
from all corners
and scorching heat.

But just as a coin is tossed,   *Luke 15:8-10 ESV
then rolls away lost…

or one sheep leave the fold   *Luke 15:4-7 ESV
with its fate so untold…

the Rightful Owner
    will comb the world
to claim
    His chosen
        treasure and pearl.   *Matthew 13:44-46 KJV

So how much more precious
is a bride,   *Ephesians 5:25-27 NKJV
despite what all
she tries to hide?

The Groom will cover every ground
till what belongs to Him is found.

He has the time and grace to wait
right up until the coming date…

and when that hour is round at last,
they'll be no longer need to fast.   *Matthew 9:15, Mark 2:19, Luke 5:34 - NIV
No darkened sky or shadows cast
will drown the call of trumpets' blast.   *Matthew 24:31, Revelation 11:15 - NASB

And once He's ventured out into
those last few streets for love that's true…   *Matthew 22:9 ESV

then wedding bells will sound   *Revelation 19:7 NKJV
so loud—
the dead will rise from ground.   *1 Thessalonians 4:16 NIV

All to witness these wedding vows
and mysteries we'll know somehow...

so she will find that Sacred Gate!   *John 10:7-9 NLT
Though she was lost, He's never late.

In Here, My Hiding Place

In here
this quiet place
door is shut
with windows, blinded…
…across the way
a mirror casts back   *1 Corinthians 13:12 NLT
the dim-hued wall
and clothes are strewn
as a lamp's light fades
from near empty oil.   *Matthew 25:8 NIV

Out here
this quiet place
I watch
the lemon-green April leaves
dawn on every branch
that sections up the sky
and yet…

-inside/out-

have all become so indiscernible
-interchangeable-
yet without change,
the monotony
of steel-gray, chain-link days
twisted
to form
yet another barrier
I cannot penetrate.

And in here,
this other
solumn assembly—

the seats are wide
with the Way
made more narrow   *Matthew Chapter 23 KJV
than It is,
and *some*
of these windows—
blinded from being
stained so much,
that there is no
Son
in this dark place.

Yet I kneel,
with impending plea...for *what?*
"Just *something* somehow please
just *let me FEEL* again!"

Then alone
in prayer
through room after room
all vacant and hollow—
it does not leave...
it hisses...
it follows me...
with the pervading weight of nothing.
How can it weigh so much?

But in here
-this private torment-
a heart still beats
as Life is breathed
into my winter   *Song of Solomon 2:11 ESV
by lips unseen,
raised up   *Psalm 145:14 KJV
by humble hands.
I cannot fathom

their strength
that lifts my
man-made cross
of nothingness
into oblivion.

And in here
my Hiding Place,   *Psalm 32:7, 91:1 NIV
I seek sweet refuge   *Psalm 18:2 NKJV
that is found again
through such a
meek and lowly Spirit   *Matthew 11:29 ESV
Who lends a hand
to offer me
His
blood-bought
Rose
of Sharon.   *Song of Solomon 2:1 NIV

*This is a poem about the living with the struggle of clinical depression, as I have experienced it. At times like these, the enemy colors our whole perception of our surroundings – causing us to potentially even loose hope in the church. But the all sufficient grace of Jesus Christ that sustains us in the darkest of times...He comes to renew our faith. He *becomes* our hope...when hope seems lost.

A Valentine, Divine

In my sorrow and my grief,
the hardest thing can be belief.

For all my fears, they plague me now
like some demented, sacred cow.   *Exodus 32:20 KJV
Have I no hope? For I feel lost,
by some seducing temptress tossed...

another god of wood and stone   *Deuteronomy 4:28 KJV
as philosophic psyches drone,

and
I am
left...all so alone,
until I bow before the Throne!   *Hebrews 4:16 NIV

For there is grace,   *2nd Corinthians 12:8-9 ESV
abounding love   *John 3:16 KJV
that cradles me...
this selfless Dove!   *Matthew 3:16, Mark 1:10, Luke 3:22, John 1:32 - KJV

He died for doubters   *John 20:24-29 NIV
just as I,
he died for those who murder, lie...   *Acts 22:4-8 NASB

and for a certain fancy few
who sit, all smiles, within the pew!   *Matthew 6:5 KJV

They never cry, never repent
they never knell or have time spent

wailing inside an inner room,   *Matthew 6:6 NASB
desperate – wanting just their Groom...   *Mark 2:19, Ephesians 5:32,
                                              Revelation 19:7 - KJV

but lie
in dungeons of key-less cages—
a prim private pain, where ever rages...

a whitewashed soul   *Matthew 23:27 NIV
and freshly painted,
picket fences, so unaquainted...

with Adonai, not yet, at least -
until comes round His final feast...   *Revelation 19:7 KJV

because His table will be filled   *Luke 14:15-24 KJV
with honest hearts   *Psalm 51:17 NIV
who've prayed until

all pride has gone before the fall   *Proverbs 16:18 ESV
of man, from God there comes a call,

"Come touch My wounds,   *Isaiah 53:5, John 20:27 - KJV
I give them here!
Come feel the pain
sin caused Me, Dear...

it is for you, that I await -
a faithful Shepherd,   *John 10:11 KJV
an open gate.   *John 10:9 NIV

And all your hate
for Me, I know
you've many questions – answered slow...

But when it is hard to see through dark,
I AM - the swift, uplifting spark...   *Exodus 13:21-22 KJV

a holy flame that ever burns,   *Matthew 3:11 KJV
and for your love, that ever yearns!

For you, I died, and love you still...   *John 3:16 KJV
but leave you now, with this, your will.

And it's your's, I will not take it...
but I call that you forsake it -   *Matthew 16:24-28 NIV

and come with Me
where 'ere I lead,
my humble flock   *John 10 :16 KJV
for you to feed...   *Luke 22:19 NASB

on just My Word   *Matthew 4:4 NIV
and Spirit more,   *John 16:7-15 ESV
Sweet Virgin Bride,   *Isaiah 62:5 KJV
I do adore...

unlike some vile and painted harlot
whose robes, once white, have become scarlet...

with incessant pleas to repent,
My blood is spilled – My anger spent...   *Isaiah 53:10 KJV

and not on you or mankind more,
but on my cross – the veil, I tore!   *Matthew 27:51 KJV

And lift your's now, for all to see
your yearning gleam, My fallen knee.

That by these wounds that set you free,
be Mine, My love, My Bride to be."   *Revelation 19:7 KJV

Darkest Before the Dawn

Street lights shine
through mini-blinds,
lighting my little room—leaving
horizontal shadow lines
against the head board.
They are comforting—remind me
life goes on
outside my four walls at night;
and these lights
shield us from
the feared darkness
that would only be
the moonlight
coming clean
as eschewed sunlight from
yesterday. Back when
we could breathe
fresh air
...when doors were left unlocked
(as Grandma claimed)
and
boys and girls
could play outside
(without drive-bys)
or pedophiles
who would
    slip through
the unforeseen cracks in
lady liberty
that now rip her
bell
up the middle
and all apart.
But back then

were also
jim crow laws
and
crosses
getting burned.
Yes, history teaches
(but do we learn)
from other dark thoughts
and consequences:
    swastikas symbolizing
    unbridled hate which fed on
    His Chosen Ones   *Deuteronomy 7:6 KJV
    like hungry fires-burning
    and churning, ravenous,
    unending, insatiable, incessant
    appetites   *1 Peter 5:8 NIV
    that sought out
    imagined enemies everywhere—a hatred
that will eventually
feed on itself someday,
will choke on
its own
rough ferocity.

So now…
where's our preverbial
Road Not Taken
to lead us
back to Virtue…
but was there ever virtue…?
If we could betray, deny, and crucify   *Matthew 27:32-56 KJV
our only Hope?   *Isaiah 42:1-4, Matthew 12:15-21 - KJV

Isn't there a safe place
where Light is brighter   *Revelation 21:23 KJV
than our electric man-made lamps

cluttered along our little roads
and a Light   *John 8:12 KJV
brighter still
than the
second rate sunshine
off our moon…
where there are
no paths
that have to be so
are straight and narrowed…   *Matthew 7:14 KJV
where
Adonai
is one with us and   *1 Corinthians 13:12 KJV
His Bright Son   *1 John 4:14-15, Revelation 22:5 - KJV
will radiate
    to light
       the Way   *John 14:6 KJV
and warm our souls?

A Place…
where darkness simply is not,
and so need not,
be feared.

Brush Strokes

a canvas, clean
a Way made plain   *John 14:6 KJV
'spite all my paint
and sin and stain

it's so pristine
so white, so pure
and cannot tempt   *James 1:13 NIV
us or allure

for it is perfect
undefiled,
and
set apart
for tempers mild

who will not trash it
at the sight
of a mistake
or coming plight

who will in modest
temperance be
content to turn   *Acts 3:19 NIV
the brush and see   *Matthew 13:16 KJV

what majesty will be created
for those who've sought
and pined
and waited   *Isaiah 40:31 ESV

for strength renewed
an eagle's wing

a walk not faint
in death, no sting   *1 Corinthians 15:55 KJV

and yet it's easy
understand
to question movements
by the hand

of the Artist's sudden plan
or so it seems
as we withstand

the disappearing grand designs
of our own thoughts and wants and minds

until we near the brink of sanity
until we see that all is vanity   *Ecclesiastes 1:2 KJV

and then surrender   *Mark 8:35 KJV
to the sight
of His perspective,   *Isaiah 55:9 KJV
hue, and Light…   *John 8:12 KJV

as these transform a lowly page
to new creation's   *2nd Corinthians 5:17 KJV
war that's waged

'gainst principalities and powers   *Ephesians 6:12-13 KJV
in every age
and passing hour

that we keep watch   *Mark 13:35 KJV
and linger much
to see
the Artist's graceful touch   *Matthew 20:33-34 KJV

from which His fingertips does flow
an eloquence in painful throes

like Mother Moses in the reeds   *Exodus 2:3 KJV
we sense a primal aching need

to see our own, from chains, now freed
as passion grows and colors bleed

poured out   *Matthew 26:28 KJV
as offering to all
to ears that hear   *Matthew 13:16 KJV
there comes a call   *Romans 11:29 KJV

to see this stoic Master peace   *Isaiah 9:6 KJV
come back to life   *1 Corinthians 15:20-27 KJV
and never cease

His work in progress as it stands   *Philippians 1:6 KJV
in stars of skies and grains of sand…   *Genesis 22:17 KJV

are burdens light and easy yokes   *Matthew 11:28-30 KJV
from His divine and guiding strokes.

The Trouble with Band-aids

*Jeremiah 6:14 KJV

A wound has occurred
and because we care,
we slap on a bandaid
and do not dare…

ever remove it
or stop to check
if it is working
or if it's a wreck.

We take for granted
that band-aids don't heal.
They only cover
our nasty ordeals.

And often times
they serve
    only to slow,
the healing process,
as infection grows.

And since we can't see
the scar as it festers,
we compound the problem
with more loving gestures.

Like new colorful band-aids
of unique design—
thinking they'll distract
us from pain, now confined.

And week after week
all our sorrows

*Mark 13:8 NIV

remain—
through ski trips and socials
and choral refrain.

We try to ignore it,
we want to pretend…
that band-aids restore it
so we can defend…

the lack of time spent
and attention paid
to the source of injury
and the mess we have made…

from smothering a cut
that runs far too deep…
saved only
    by blood

      coming soon   *Revelation 22:7-12 KJV
            as it seeps…

in gradual expense
through the bandage, it keeps
spilling out to cleanse
the disease that we reap…   *Galatians 6:7 KJV

after leaving thin gauze
that's repeatedly dunked
in water, lukewarm,   *Revelation 3:15-17 KJV
with the stench of a skunk.

Til we are
Abel   *Genesis 4:4 KJV
to see   *Matthew 13:16 KJV
    a new course

of *action* to heal
this wound at its source,

and rip off the band-aids
from top to bottom,
with a burning of flesh
that will rival old Sodom!   *Genesis Chapter 19 KJV

But first, call the Doctor...   *Matthew 9:12 KJV
the One in the Book
and lend wounds over
to *Him*
for a look.

He will tell you the Truth,   *John 14:6 KJV
that wounds should be exposed...
to the Bright Morning Light   *Revelation 22:16 KJV
and fresh scent
      of a Rose.   *Song of Solomon 2:1 KJV

An Answer to His Child

I've run from God and hid my face   *Isaiah 53:3 KJV
in sin, despair, and deep disgrace...

into a corner, dark and cold,
as night rolls in and darkness told...

me all the reasons for my shame
that I am lost, no one to blame.

And yet a tender whisper calls   *1st Kings 19:12 KJV
from deep within my prison walls...

"Your Advocate   *1 John 2:1 KJV
Physician, Great...   *Luke 5:31-31 KJV

Your Shepherd, Good   *John 10:11-15 KJV
And Sacred Gate...   *John 10:9 KJV

I know you   *John 10:14 KJV
hunger
I know you
thirst   *Matthew 5:6 KJV

I know you,
child of Adam, cursed.   *Genesis 3:16-19, Romans 5:19 - KJV

So know this now,
your case I plead.

Know I AM all
you'll ever need.   *2 Peter 1:3 KJV

The Bread of Life   *John 6:35 KJV
and water, living...   *John 4:7-30 KJV

sufficient grace--   *2nd Corinthians 12:9 KJV
your sin, forgiving …   *1 John 1:9 KJV

It is for you
I came to die,   *John 3:16 KJV
and hunger - thirst,
I satisfy…   *Psalm 107:9 KJV

I call to you, "Come, follow Me…"   *Matthew 16:24 KJV
from virgin womb and hallowed tree, *Isaiah 7:14; Matthew 1:23 KJV

to die to self and turn from sin
and rise with Me, anew, again…   *Romans 6:8 KJV

straight to that dark and desperate day
when I return and have My Way…

when the world is filled with Godly sorrow
once and for all, this yet, tomorrow…

when skies turn to sackcloth, black *Revelation 6:12 KJV
with the moon as blood - I'm coming back *Revelation 22:20 KJV

for all that's Mine, for everything, *Psalm 50:10-12 KJV
I spoke to life 'mid seraph wings *Genesis Chapter 1 KJV

with eyes aflame that search for you, *Revelation 19:12 KJV
My darling bride, My love that's true." *Ephesians 5:32 KJV

Abraham's Rainbow

I drove to the beach today.
It seemed a
waste of sunshine
not to go,
because it had been raining
so I hoped to see
a great rainbow.

*Genesis 9:13-16 KJV

And there I spotted
a caramel-colored woman
with dark, almond-shaped eyes.
Her long hair reached
the small of her back
and is just as course and thick
as mine, but even at the ends
and coal black—darker than my own.
Two tiny crosses of silver
reflect the Son
in each of her ears.

Then I notice another lady
at the water's edge.
Her skin reminds me of
bitter-sweet dark chocolate.
She's wearing a one-piece swimsuit
with a marble gray-white pattern,
and her long, exotic braids
dance freely about her shoulders.
She's walking with a man
as dark as ebony.
From his broad shoulders
down to the middle of his being
sways a cross of gold
that's big enough to bear.

And he caught my cap
as it blew past
like any
Good Samaritan.   *Luke 10:25-37 KJV

One young girl
has coal black waves
that reach her elbows, and
the six-pointed
Star of David
dangles from round
her dainty neck.

One guy is wearing
full-length camouflage trousers
but cannot hide
with his tattoos of all variety,
one of Christ's crucifixion.
(We bleed for what we love.)
His skin is alabaster
not white like a sheet…
but a ghost—*familiar*   *Acts 2:38 KJV
to me,
somehow.

My own skin is ivory,
but turning
into a painful pink.
Pain means change,   *Romans 5:3-5 KJV
and I should
no doubt
darken up in days
into a healthy tan
like my grandpa had.
His skin was olive
and of Cheyenne descent…

though my grandma's name
was Patterson,
and she had
green Irish eyes
that read the Bible
to me
from a rocking chair.

But now all of us
have converged
at the edge
of the water today.

Some jump in headlong,
while others wade a while.

I step gradually,
waiting for each
impending wave.

But a lukewarm splash
just *sickens* me,   *Revelation 3:16 KJV
so I head further out—
I want to roll
with bigger waves.
They come in high and hard.
But that gets boring fast,
because the water is so soft,
moving through me,
so I wait for the next big wave...
and when it comes
I float freely
on top of its crest.
And after that I soon felt
the safe floor of wet sand
beneath my feet.

Craving yet more excitement,
I throw myself into
the next wave
and it slaps my torso. Undaunted,
I run faster into the next,
defiant—over confident.
And this next wave was bigger
than I'd intended.
It grabbed my tip toes
out from under me
and its crest lapped
over my head,
left my frail pail body
helpless under
its mounting weight,
and my mouth left
gaping out of breath
and underwater…
being thrown back like
a fisherman's reject,   *Matthew 4:19 KJV
tossed roughly
but safely against the shore
with a vicious case of sand-burn
and
the sickly tart taste
from the
salt of the earth   *Matthew 5:13-16 KJV
and the sea
in my throat.

Still…I went back again,
humbled,   *Proverbs 3:34 KJV
just content to float
for a bit
atop the waves.

Despite my obvious
failure at sea
I knew
my Older Brother Who'd   *Hebrews 2:11-18 KJV
gone before me
-further out-
into the *deep*   *Luke 5:4, John 21:6 KJV
and was there to save me,   *Luke 9:56 KJV
could
walk on water   *Matthew 14:25 KJV
if He had to.

So I just HAD to get this right,
I spot another roller coaster wave
and let it consume me,
fell helpless backward with it,
let it wash me,
held my breath
as it pulled me under,
ignoring the stinging stench
of salt water sneaking
into my left nostril
and the burning in my lungs.

For that one moment
I felt as one
with the ocean
and nature,
in submission to it all   *James 4:7 KJV
and the LORD Himself
until the wave
sat me
on the shore
to see
around some more.

Happy-go-lucky people
by the thousands now
were still
clustered all around
at hotdog stands
on roller blades
and bikes cycling,
weaving smoothly
in and out
just like the waves
that move the wading masses.
I hated to leave
this unique paradise.

Sadly I noticed that the sky
had offered no rainbow,
but I couldn't be disappointed
with so many multi-colored
umbrella tops bowed up
to stake out
billions of different little
claims and cultures…
the LORD's *promise,*   *Galatians 3:15-18 KJV
after all.

Author's Note:
Truly, Noah was not the only servant of our LORD who was given a
rainbow. For to Abraham was promised descendants as numerous as the
stars of the skies and the sands of the oceans!

Be Still and Know

Be still and know
that
I AM   *Exodus 3:14 KJV
there,
in all moments
fully aware.   *Psalm 147:5, Isaiah 40:28 - KJV

Be still and know
that
I AM   *Luke 14:62 KJV
He,
Who died for you   *1 Peter2:21-25 KJV
on Calvary's Tree.   *Galatians 3:13 KJV

Be still and know
that for this reason,
that
I AM   *John 6:35; 8:12; 10:9, 11; 11:25-26; 14:6; 15:5 - KJV
with you   *Matthew 28:20 KJV
through all seasons.   *Ecclesiastes 3:1-8 KJV

Be still and know
I rule the grave...   *1st Corinthians 15:24-26, *Revelation 1:18 KJV
it does not keep
the ones I save!

Be still and know
that
I AM
near,   *James 4:8 KJV
'spite all your angst
and nervous fear.

Be still and know
I AM
the Way,
the Truth, and Life   *John 14:6 KJV
and that I stay...

deep within your
conscious soul,   *1st Corinthians 3:16 KJV
your groaning cries   *Romans 8:26 KJV
that take a role...

above Me
~in your heart~
some, now and then--
yet I'll forgive
this present sin...

that separates us
to My grief;
for I can offer
sweet relief...

from all your pain
and heartache so,
it is important
that you know...

My passion for you, Bride,   *Ephesians 5:32, Revelation 19:7 - KJV
is new--
and My commitment
tried and true!

I see that all my sheep are fed,   *John 21:17 KJV
not left to starve or even dread...

but cast their cares
on Me instead,
as every page
they've turned and read...

*Psalm 55:22, 1 Peter 5:7 KJV

of My bold words
and pious claims--
so rest assured
I AM
the same.

*Hebrews 13:8 KJV

Look now to My
strong staff and rod.

*Psalm 23:4 KJV

Be still and know
that I AM God.

Be Ye Holy

Set apart,   *Jeremiah 1:5 KJV
He has you called by name...   *Isaiah 43:1 KJV
no more
grieving, endless shame.   *Revelation 21:4 KJV

Set apart,
He has made you whole...   *Mark 5:34 KJV
no more
straying from the fold.   *Luke 15:1-7 KJV

Set apart,   *1 Peter 5:13-15 KJV
He has brought you to life...   *Romans 6:4 KJV
no more
fear of death and strife.   *1 Corinthians 15:55, 2 Timothy 1:10 - KJV

Consecrated,
once and for all
by His choice   *Ephesians 1:4 KJV
'spite Adam's fall.   *Genesis 3 KJV

Consecrated,
you have been
given victory   *1 Corinthians 15:57 KJV
over sin.

Consecrated,
you are made pure   *Isaiah 1:18 KJV
by the wounds
He did endure.   *Isaiah 53:5 1 Peter 2:24 KJV

HOLY   *1 Peter 1:16 KJV
no wrinkle, spot, or blemish...   *Ephesians 5:27 KJV
we'll base eternity
on this premise:

God loves the world so,   *John 3:16 KJV
that angels sing…   *Luke 2:13-14 KJV
about the ransom   *Matthew 20:28, Luke 10:45 KJV
of our King!   *John 18:37, Revelation 19:16 KJV

"By Mother's Grave"

For my dear, late mother-in-law ~ Pat Todd

Loss and grief,
fear and strife...
money spent
and my life
is out of dreams,
ambition dies
as night crawls round
and family ties
are in the ground
no more to be
a sheltering voice
that comforts me...
reminding of
a childhood home
where cares were few
no need to roam.
But now I'm grown
and you are gone
as memories fade
within the dawn...
of a new day with troubles new,
problems to solve and things to do.
But like a dream upon the wake,
your essence comes just for my sake—
surrounding me and all my senses!
The scent of you strips my defenses,
and leaves me bare, bereft, undone.
Nowhere to hide, no way to run.
And if I could, why would I leave?
If this all I've left to grieve?
A glimpse of you, a shadow past
returns to me and at long last.
Your whisper rough, but faint I feel

and pine for times when it seems real.
You acted well, your role as sage
if all the world is just a stage...

playing your Naomi to my Ruth,   Ruth 1:16-17 ESV
I clung to you, sayer of sooth...
who told me that our LORD is good—
that faith to keep, of this I should.
And that I did, your God was mine!
So I will see you again sometime...
when you are new and whole again,
apart from death and pain and grievous sin.
Though our vile bodies, all will perish,
and leave only cold stones to cherish—
we will be raised, restored, equipped
Into our heavenly citizenship!   *Philippians 3:20-21 ESV
Where cancer can no longer thrive—
where we are with the Christ, *alive!*
So when He comes with outstretched hand,
I know just where I want to stand...
right at the sight of One Who Saves,
I want to be...by our mom's grave.

I AM

Where are You, God?
In my aches and pain...
the constant groaning,   *Romans 8:26-27 ESV
driving me insane.

Where are You, God?
When I'm alone...
can You hear me
from Your throne?

Where are You, God?
In my loss and fear...
I draw close to You,
but are You near?   *James 4:8 ESV

"My child, I AM
your present Friend,   *John 15:15 ESV
your God, your Father
til the end.

I AM the wind   *John 3:8 NKJV
that comforts you.   *John 14:16 NKJV
I AM the sweet
fresh fallen dew.   *Deuteronomy 32:2 ESV

I AM the dawn
of a new day,
where mercy's new   *Lamentations 3:22-24 ESV
and fear's at bay.

I AM the Waker   *Revelation 3:2 NKJV
and the Keep   *Psalm 121:5 NASB
of those you love
who've gone asleep!   *Ephesians 5:14 NIV, 1 Corinthians 15:51 ESV

I AM the spring
in bloom for you,   *Hosea 6:3 NASB
I AM the change
that makes you new.   *Revelation 21:5 NLT

I AM the rich
redeeming blood,   *Ephesians 1:7 ESV
I AM the fast
swift-coming flood!   *Matthew 24:36-39 NIV; Luke 17:26-27 NIV

I AM the song   *Psalm 118:14 ESV; Isaiah 12:2 ESV
that makes you sing.
I AM your Groom,   *Ephesians 5:22-33 NKJV
you have My ring.

I AM the first,
I AM the last   *Revelation 22:13 NKJV
onto Whom
your cares now cast!   *1 Peter 5:7 NKJV

I AM the One
upon the cross.
I AM your *hope…*   *1 Peter 1:3-5 NIV
when hope seems lost."

Faith Has Made You

When everything is lost and wrong...
when night is dark and day is long...

my soul screams out from constant pain
I call to You throughout the strain ...

and it is You Who gives me rest,   *Matthew 11:28 NIV
not those who claim to know God's best,

for in Your Word, you said there'd be
this suffering and desperate pleas   *Psalm 34:19 ESV

to know You more each passing day,   *Colossians 1:9 NKJV
to chase You down like jars of clay   *Jeremiah 18:1-11 ESV

who need the Potter's steady hand   *Isaiah 45:9 NIV
-like stars at night, like grains of sand-   *Genesis 22:17 NIV

so numerous and yet diverse...
set us apart,   *1 Peter 2:9 ESV
and break a curse;   *Romans 5:12-17 ESV

so that in all we do or claim,
we glorify Your holy name...   *1 Corinthians 10:31 NIV

to show that You have played a role
in broken lives who're now made whole!

some say I'm not jealous,   *Exodus 20:5 NLT
but I assure you

I AM   *Exodus 3:14 NASB, Mark 14:62 NLT

some say I'm not zealous,   *Isaiah 42:8 NASB
but for My children

I AM

you say that you're bored
and tired of My Way,
that you want to go
to a friend's house and play

and so,
      I won't force you
my child,
      won't divorce you

I give you
      some free will
            to decide

with whom you will go
but I want you to know

I'll be waiting
      'til your back
            by My side   *Romans 11:25-29 NKJV

and don't be surprised
at the tears in My eyes   *Luke 19:41-42 ESV
when some new
      father figure

43

comes along
and him, you adore—
for his rules aren't a chore
but what
he feeds you
won't make you grow strong

yes, he'll let you play
however you may…

out in the streets,
no buckles for seats
no homework, bedtime
no reasons, no rhyme
    and your wish will be his command
and whatever you say
is his rule for the day
    but for you, he won't take a stand

he's there to be "fun"
and your heart, he's won
    by telling you what you want to hear
but he does not care
about your welfare
    and has made that abundantly clear

then you come
    back to Me,
with broken bones
bloody knees
from a weekend of having
    your own way
without My Truth
for My Life to give proof
    that you would have been wiser to stay

some say I'm not jealous,
but I assure you

I AM

some say I'm not zealous
but for My children

I AM

and for this there are many good reasons
though times will change
and customs rearrange
I remain as a constant in all seasons   *Hebrews 13:8 KJV

so whether you love Me
or curse My name
this simple truth
is always the same

I AM

the beginning,
and

I AM
the end—   *Revelation 22:13 NIV
and I love you so much
that My Son I did send…   *John 3:16 NIV

so make it apparent

I AM

a faithful, *firm* parent
and as such,
My love
     never ends.   *Psalm 100:5 NIV

Christ's bride   *Ephesians 5:22-33 NKJV
has slept,
while He's waited and wept—   *Luke 19:41 NIV
    but death, now it has no sing…   *1 Corinthians 15:55 ESV
And I do strive
knowing she will survive
and will waken   *Ephesians 5:14 NIV
    when called by her King.   *Revelation 3:2 NIV

For **I AM**   *Exodus 3:14 ESV, Mark 14:52 NLT
   JUST   *John 5:30 ESV
   …as a Servant—   *Mark 10:45 NASB
   in all this time gone by.
And though the house
is unclean   *Isaiah 64:6 NASB
that doesn't mean
   I've quit or haven't tried.

I'd no fancy robes   *Mark 12:38 NASB; Luke 20:46 NASB
from distant parts of the globe
   I donned a servant's towel
and My hands did get dirty
washing feet   *John 13:5-15 NIV
cracked and hurting
   all with a smile, not a scowl.

And there is only one dress   *Revelation 19:8 NIV
once perfect and pressed
   fit for a great wedding, that's true.   *Revelation 19:7-9 NIV
But now it's a mess
and no one will confess
   as to how
      it's been *stained* and *misused*.

Dirty laundry
piles high,
and I field heavy sighs…
    one complaint after another.
I still come to help
though asking Myself,
    "Why can't they be more
        like their Brother!"   *Hebrews 2:11-12 NIV

But
   I AM
      here to sweep away
      the ash   *Isaiah 61:3 NIV
      from trays
      and to *scatter*   *Luke 1:51 ESV
      the dust   *Genesis 3:19 NIV
      and matter
from tables---*turned*,   *Matthew 21:12 NASB; John 2:15 NASB
no lessons learned…

…and
   I AM
by some ignored,
considered a bore

left stuffed in a shelf
-beside Myself-
while some family members
can't even remember
My heartfelt convictions
and painful afflictions
they disregard My opinions
and enjoy their dominion
over the earth
to whom I gave birth

and what was it worth
if not for My mirth…?

Since rain must fall   *Matthew 5:45 NIV
upon you all
from time to time
in My reason and rhyme…

if
I AM
in My *wealth*   *Isaiah 33:6, NASB
still stuck in your shelves,
then you'll have to
pick up after yourselves.

For dirt will pile up—
passing plates,
    filthy cups   *Matthew 23:25 NIV; Luke 11:39 NIV
      that cannot be filled,
by your own works   *Galatians 5:19-21 NIV
and anxious quirks
    until you can learn to be still…   *Psalm 46:10 ESV

and know
    what *Way*
      the *Truth* will stay
        with the *Life*   *John 14:6 NASB
you are living:
for you must keep forgiving   *Matthew 18:21-22 NKJV
and stop reliving

all your past pain
that drives you insane,
but give it to Me
and you will see   *Matthew 13:16 NKJV

that the force of My Living Water,   *John 4:7-13 NIV
hot   *Revelation 3:15 NIV
-as iron in the solder-   *Malachi 3:2-3 NKJV

will wash pain
down the drain
with no worry   *Matthew 6:27; Luke 12:25 NIV
      to remain…

then keep on going
strong and growing
      like orchard trees
neat in a row
with fruit to show   *Revelation 22:2 NIV
      that's grown ripe
            to disperse the seeds…   *Matthew 13:3-8 NLT

-so that the world-

…with hope diminished
can be replenished
from work that's been *finished,*   *John 19:30 ESV
complete—and as pure as Lamb's fleece.
Though consequences, infernal;
and housework, eternal;
strength comes from an internal peace…

…to surpass understanding   *Philippians 4:7 ESV
through troubles demanding
attention, time-spent, and tolls taken—

you'll have great delight   *Psalm 37:4 NASB
to fight the good fight   *1 Timothy 6:12 NIV
for the pride of My joy
      when she wakens!   *Ephesians 5:14 ESV

I Seldom Pray for Miracles

I seldom pray for miracles,
not because I don't believe.

I seldom pray for miracles,
for I hope not to receive...

blessings that I don't deserve
for I, have nothing done...

for that so precious of a grace
my human heart has won.

In me - there is nothing;
I am apart...undone,

save for my Master and His face
that's shone in Christ, the Son.

I seldom pray for miracles,
because, you see, I feel...

that if I pine for health and wealth
the enemy might steal...

all the love I have for Christ,
without Whom – I'd be lost.

I seldom pray for miracles...
I have one...on the *cross*.

King Herod's Last Strike

*Genesis 3:15 ESV

I watched a tv show last night
about abortion, our *civil* right.

> A sweet young girl lay
> on a table, chewing bubble gum,
> while a doctor—as requested
> used a machine that hummed.
> It ground and churned inside her,
> I bet it made her bleed.
> And she was shaken,
> crying endlessly.
> "It must have hurt," I cried
> *with her*
> while sitting home, unseen.

And
I AM
angry at king herod   *Matthew 2:16 ESV
who is now disguised
as the desperation
that's been
eating this girl alive.

You see, king herod
drinks his wine, screams—
"All for me, me, me!"
He does not share with anyone,
it's good to be the 'king.'

And king herod continues
to rear his ugly head
in third world famines,
plagues, and pestilence.

Then he visits every land
with needles and cocaine,
all targeted toward the children
just to see if they'll refrain.
Or maybe they'll fall
into his elusive trap…
overdose or HIV,
both prospects on his map.

I've learned king herod
will change his form   *2 Corinthians 11:14 NIV
from one century to another,
appearing out of nowhere
through come cause,
disease, or mother.

The children are the LORD's favored,   *Matthew 18:3-4 NLT
as we're told in His petition.
So every age this old king herod
tries to squelch the competition.

You see, king herod
is a *serpent*
of the lowest breed.   *Genesis 3:14 ESV
He cons and wheels and deals…
and on our souls, he feeds.   *1 Peter 5:8 NASB

You know,
I think he is *afraid*
that his reign
will soon be up.
I think he knows,

Someone is coming…   *Revelation 22:12 NIV

with
Wine His Own
to flow over
all our cups.

*1 Corinthians 11:25 NIV

*Psalm 23:5 ESV

Letting Go

You were so small
when handed to me
-dark purple and still-
you barely breathed.

I hardly did, too...
while waiting to see
why you didn't cry
or move suddenly.

I held you tight,
I wouldn't let go
in that first moment
unable to know...

just what you needed
or how to find it—
that first of many moments,
if I could rewind it...

would I have you again?
Knowing how it's been...

so hard for you
in a world
you can't choose...

where crowds upset you
and people stare,
where words are like
a den of snares

that trap and snag you
in their maze,

while you wrestle
from a daze

they leave you hanging
on pieces gleaning,
as you struggle
with gestures for meaning...

something wanted
something found
something lost
or some strange sound

...has sent you wailing
high and low...
I hold you tight,
I won't let go.

How to ease your pain
I seldom know,
but I hold you tight
and won't let go.

I brace for impact,
weather the storm—
just to keep you
safe from harm.

But have you again?
Of course, I sure would!
For one of your smiles
shines like the sun *should.*

And for all of the blessings
that came by surprise,

as it was *through you* that
Christ opened my eyes…

and showed me the point
of life as we know it—
to lean on His grace,   2nd Corinthians 12:9-10
letting His power show it…

to reach out to others
and to lift them up high,
not shrink from our problems
or shake fists at the sky.

And that's not to say
it's all been a breeze,
for I've spent many nights
bent down on my knees…

asking Him, *"WHY?!*
Was it something *I* did?
To deserve this lot,
what crime have I hid?

Have I passed down
my sin to *you?"*
I ask Him, *"Please!"*
That it's not true!

And in His Word,
I have found rest.*   *Matthew 11:28 ESV
It's so that He'll
be made manifest!*   *John 9:3 KJV

And that, He is
everyday—

when prayer and praise
chase fears away...

when JOY is found
on cloudy days,
that is just when
I feel Him say:

"There's just one thing
that you should know—
I AM
holding tight,
I won't let go."   *Isaiah 41:10,13 NLT

Revelations Near Midnight

imagined importance
in emerald-studded everythings
our world
a tiny scope—the centromere
of wanton emotions
and frivolous things
like so many dominoes
-like people and
the games they play-
inside gated lives
so rich with boundaries,
caged in
illusive empires
afforded for
all eyes to see
and to shed light
from a luciferin source
dimly lit
by blue-green chandelier tip
reflections,
flickering (snickering)
but bright enough
to attract
like aurora borealis
beckoning
a writhing sea
into the dark and cold
unknown, unfamiliar channels, an abyss
so hollow, void like
contracts signed
on dotted lines
and sold
in the nick of time
as waves roll overhead

submerging
-in too deep-
completely WASHED
and yet unclean
guided by an age-old
lucid arch angel
that drifts among us
seamlessly
through crimson and lavender oils
so refined,
above reproach
are these horrible things
let to stand
inside the temple
where incantation
smoke is blown
incensed
to hypnotize
the wading masses
of devout followers,
undaunted despite
Truth   *John 14:6 ESV
and heirs to the
Kingdom of Heaven
who cry out
with no one to suffer them
or rival perceived authority
not to mention
bloody clinic floors
and battlefields of
no less consequence
these
reigning cats and dogs
will have their moment
in the limelight

...quite apart
from the Son...

with no mortal wind
strong enough to
sweep away the
wicked witches
of the east
or the west
where forest fires devour
and mud slides sour, sloping
downward into homelessness
and diseased apathy of
laissez-faire campaigns
that got US over a barrel
of crude complaints
and black sheep's wool
pulled over eyes
already blind,
lost
and lacking
any focus...

...how I welcome baptismal floods
of Living Water   *John 7:38 NIV
in a deluge bursting free
from all the damned and disenchanted,
ripping through
our stony fortress, leaving no one
left
to lie.

My Surrendering

Take all that's in me which You hate,
and crush it for Your Kingdom's sake:
vanity   *Ecclesiastes 1:2 ESV
and selfish pride,   *Proverbs 16:18 NLT
anger,   *Ephesians 4:26-27 NIV
lust—   *1 John 2:16 NASB
my soul divide,
split it clean
and make me whole,
that I may someday
play a role...

in Your grand and Great Commission   *Matthew 28:18-20 NASB
to call a world for sin's remission.   *Matthew 26:28 KJV

For all who knock, Your open door;   *Luke 11:9 NIV
and all who ask, You've given more: *Matthew 25:29 NIV

as Sarah laughed in her old age—   *Genesis 18:12 NASB
You gave a son, nations, to raise.   *Genesis 21:1-5 NASB

as Moses begged to stay your wrath   *Exodus 32:11-14 NIV
from Israelites who chose a calf...   *Exodus 32:1-4 NIV

as Joshua spoke, the sun stood still;
and moon did stop, all at Your will...   *Joshua 10 NASB

as Gideon asked for dew-filled fleece,
You showered it and gave him peace...   *Judges 6 NLT

as Ruth clung to Naomi—*spent*,   *Ruth 1:14 ESV
You gave her Boaz, royal descent...   *Ruth 4:13-17 ESV

as Samuel said, "...Your servant hears..."   *1 Samuel 3:9 NIV
You prophesied & drew him near...

as Elijah fled and made his choice,
You came to him in a still, small voice!   *1 Kings 19:12 KJV

So search my heart and soul and mind—   *Psalm 139:23 NASB
and give me grace, oh God, divine.
Open my eyes   *Matthew 13:16 ESV
and these wounds, bind;   *Psalm 147:3 ESV
for
I am
seeking, sure to find...   *Matthew 7:7 NIV

a *treasure* hidden in a field;   *Matthew 13:44 ESV
a *pearl* of price no one can steal!   *Matthew 13:45 ESV

For, as I delight myself in You,   *Psalm 37:4 NASB
You will
change my heart
and make it true...

to Your Holy Word and Him, alone,   *John 1:1-4 ESV
that I cast all crowns before His Throne!   *Revelation 4:10-11 NASB

Shadow Dancer

A waif gray image
that's caught a ride,
and follows after—
but has to hide,

having no real life
of its own
content to race
around unknown.

Chasing after any man
depending on…
    where he stands:

in the Light   *John 3:19 ESV
or shady play,
in the street
or in the Way.   *Acts 24:14 NIV

For in the Light   *John 8:12 NLT
it can't be found,
but let Light fade
and it abounds.

The shadow dancer
scampers round—
seeking what
it hasn't found…

through wayward gates,
open and flirtin'
where nothing's long
and nothing's certain.

Getting bounced
'gainst walls or tossed,
across the ground
and often lost.

Appearing again
from nowhere to stand,
"Jump, fetch, or sit…"
on some command.

But shadows really
deserve much more—
to become real,
and holy adored.

So what then would
that dancer be
part from the chase
of feet and knees?
What could
sustain her
so fully…
but the *salvation*
of being free?   *John 8:31-21 NASB

For God made woman
from and for
a man's side…   *Genesis 2:21-24
not from some shadow
to be *cast aside.*

Last Days

Wolves come in packs,   *Matthew 7:15 ESV
thieves hide in dens—
quite in disguise
above all sin.

A multitude,
they do devour—
making a mockery
of Higher Power...

with crosses of wood & stone   *Revelation 9:20 NIV
-for looks alone-
they've crafted
into images so graven—   *Exodus 20:3-4 KJV
and truth lies
thrown
into the dirt,
coiled up and badly shaven.

Their nasty mess
has been confused
into our microphones,
as Judgment waits
at Heaven's gate
when wrath flies from the Throne.   *Matthew 10:15 NLT

But mighty oaks   *Isaiah 61:3 NASB
of easy yokes   *Matthew 11:30 KJV
stand firm against the quake—
no wind or hail
or tempest gale
can make their branches break.

Their stance is strong
with limbs grown long
and full of *fruit,*   *Galatians 5:22-23 NLT
    they render…
a wood grain
*new**   *2nd Corinthians 5:17
and fit for use
by quite a Great Carpenter.   *Matthew 13:55, Mark 6:3 - NIV

Their roots runs deep   *Jeremiah 17:8 NASB
as Water seeps   *John 7:38 NASB
up to outstretched ends—
to quench a thirst   *Matthw 5:6 NIV
for righteous works
and Truth,   *John 14:6 NIV
they will defend…

…until the day
when the Son's Light may   *Revelation 21:23 NIV
outshine the dark campaigns,
    and renew
this world unglued
with His *everlasting* reign.   *Revelation 22:5 ESV

In Cinderella's Hour

raw and white-gray
are the ashes today as
smoke is blown
from faces nearby,
as pass time is made of
flicking cinders
at death's door
while
white water falls
down from
the heartland, beating still—
holding its breath
and beholding beauty,
in awe of
witchever's work
will bring them prosperity
each hour psychic's
nickel & dime
the desperate to death,
all seeking only
    that sixth grammy
    that sixth sweet sugar pill
    that sixth stolen ego, bought & sold   *Revelation 13:18 NIV
but none for me, see
I spend my day
keeping doctors at bay
with their sufficient bedside manner
as the nurses hover
while their hair—whether
    black, brown, red, gold, or white
eclipses a distant hall light,
creating halos
that shine brightly
about their

bobbie pins and butterfly clips,
as compassionate eyes
search for
an outstretched vein
in vain
to fill a vial, vile
deed that's been done—
    been transferred,
    out of home,
    been alienated,
    bought & sold,
    like so many acres,
    like distant generations, and…
…I watch the needle
steal my blood—a stick, a prick
and off to the left,
the east,
where the wicked live
I see that
money has changed hands
again, changed two faces
into one
behind a podium
as invisible cauls
fall over expressions
promising 2nd sight,
words stirred by silver spoons
and silver tongues
are stained by them.
Civil shovels
bury the truth
leaving only their
lucrative make-believe
sickening music pipes
on and around we go on
wooden horses

up and down…
…as blood is found,
spurting in and filling up—
then the needle's taken out
by miscellaneous hands
in the early morning
and miscellaneous faces
by flashlights in the night—
all bearing gentle, gentile smiles
and sympathetic eyes
unlike
the snake eyes
of the great pretenders…
and me,
a lowly leper
who cannot change her spots,
in need of a healing touch
to make me whole again,
afforded barely
through
the *salt*   *Matthew 5:13 NIV
of the earth.

Just Cause

The Advocate,   *1 John 2:1 NIV
He pleads my case...
I cannot look upon
His face.   *Exodus 33:20 KJV

For
I am
hidden   *Exodus 33:22 NASB
in the Rock   *Matthew 21:42 ESV
-set apart-
amid the flock.

And there I wait   *Isaiah 40:31 ESV
and pine for Love
with grace sufficient   *2nd Corinthians 12:9 NIV
from above...

this hellacious world
we know;
this pain we feel,
this hurt in tow...

that snares and binds us
as we speak
from which there seems
no soon relief.

But in Him there is joy profound,   *John 15:11 NASB
a truth so told, a strength renowned—   *Psalm 28:8 NIV

that passes by...
while our heads bow,
through wind and quake and fire   *1 Kings 19:11-13 NASB
their sound-

He was not in them,
we now see
a gentle Lamb...   *1 Peter 1:19 ESV
a hallowed Tree

A Shepherd still,   *John 10:11 KJV
an open Gate   *John 10:9 NIV
Who stands before
the Magistrate

He speaks upon our own behalf;
He bids us bring the fattened calf,   *Luke 15:11-32 NASB

and celebrate
a child's return...
a soul now saved,
a lesson learned.

And so to He Who
intercedes,   *Hebrews 7:25 NASB
I fall, I cry
from on my knees -

You saved me from immortal doom,
You came despite we had no room;   *Luke 2:7 NASB

for You, forsaken, beaten – torn,
for sinner's sake, we wail and mourn!

But *revel* in
Your risen state,
Right Hand of God,   *Mark 16:19 NASB
this is Your fate:

Born as a man
from virgin womb,   *Luke 1:26-28 ESV

cast aside
within a tomb…   *Matthew 27:60 NIV

to rise again,   *Luke 24:5-6 NIV
to raise the dead   *1 Corinthians 15:52 NLT
to make us new,   *2 Corinthians 5:17 ESV
Your bride to wed…   *Revelation 19:17 NASB

on a white horse,   *Revelation 19:11 NASB
Your eyes aflame   *Revelation 19:12 NASB
we all will see Your written name…
as
"KING OF KINGS & Lord OF LordS"   *Revelation 19:16 NASB
with rod of iron and a sharp sword…   *Revelation 19:15 NASB

You'll rule not as a
Lamb Who beckons,
but as a JUDGE
   Who's come
      to reckon.

Olive Branches
(Romans 11:24)

A burning bush,   *Exodus 3:2 NASB
handwritten wall,   *Daniel 5:5-1525-26 NASB
a raving man
we once called Saul…   *Acts 22:6-16 ESV

his words to Rome,
Esphesians' note,   *Ephesians 1:2 NIV
still Word of God
whispered
by rote.

And so - a question,
popped in time,   *2nd Corinthians 11:2 ESV
in answer to
that age old crime…

of Eve's for listening far too close   *Genesis 3:1 KJV
to voices other than the Most

great kniving sword   *Hebrews 4:12 NIV
that cuts us clean…

the pain, we feel,
but Truth is gleaned!

It separates my mind and heart,
my world it rocks & tears apart…

…sweet cunning lies
down to my marrow,
as I,
the falling of all sparrows,   *Matthew 10:29-31 NASB
but saved by Christ

& ways made narrow!   *Matthew 7:14 KJV
Along this road,
I take a harrow...   *Isaiah 28:23-29 NASB

and till the ground
to make it supple,
for seeds of faith   *Matthew 13:23 NIV
with which to couple...

the emptiness, we are, alone
-apart from Him, so unatoned-

but haunted by a Holy Ghost,   *2nd Timothy 1:13-14 KJV
Who begs us pause...
Whose grace we host...

entertaining angels, unaware -   *Hebrews 13:2 ESV
that it is He,
from Whom they share

a gracious smile, a loving heart
that judges not,   *Matthew 7:1-3 KJV
but sets apart   *Leviticus 20:26 NASB

the purpose of a smooth white stone,   *Revelation 2:17 NIV
that's offered - costly - from the Throne...   *Luke 14:25-33 NIV

the Father's love,
the Son He sent...   *John 3:16 KJV
a daughter, lost, who won't repent   *Lamentations 2:18 NASB
but wails and cries,
her virtue spent...

as evil rears it's ugly head -   *Revelation 13:1 KJV
forever asking,
"Hath God said...?"   *Genesis 3:1 KJV

But still He holds an outstretched hand
a question posed, an offer stands...

"Come take His now, Sweet Child of Zion,
Come hear the roar of Judah's Lion..."   *Revelation 5:5 NLT

and Him alone, a stranger not,   *John 10:27 NIV
for Who has died and risen – thought...   *1st Thessalonians 4:14 ESV

you were His bride and are yet still;
for *you* His pilgrimage and will...

compels you, stinging night and day,
like a love lost, once gone astray...

but fated now, sweet destiny
to see and hear Him, Groom to be.

And not for Zion, all alone,
but for the gentiles' old dry bones...   *Ezekiel 37:1-14 NASB

that rise to everlasting life,
comprising now His wakened wife... *Isaiah 52:1-2 NASB, Romans 13:11 ESV

who will in full, sweet virtue be...
and taste the fruit of Calvary's Tree!   *Matthew 27:33, Mark 15:22,
                                               Luke 23:33, John 19:17 - KJV

Sons of Shame

Mephibosheth,   *2 Samuel 9 ESV
of broken frame,
there is no honor
in your name!

A father killed,
and legs now lame -
a curse from which
you must have came...

or so was feared
by one and all,
when young King David
came to call...

and seek you out
on whom to pour
God's sweet love
& blessings more!

From brokenness you did ascend
on eagle's wings, pure as the wind   *Isaiah 40:31, John 3:8 NASB

that blew you back to life again
from a dead dog to man and then   *2 Samuel 9:8 ESV

you sat within sweet cedar walls,
as distinguished heir of Saul!   *2 Samuel 9:9 ESV

And like him yet
we all will be
for those partaking
of the Tree...   *Revelation 2:7 NIV

of Life, in death
there is no hold -
that can
withstand...
this truth be told!

From mouths of babes
and prophets old,
lame legs will run
on streets of gold!   *Revelation 21:21 NASB

Blind eyes will see
deaf ears will hear   *Isaiah 35:5 NASB
the glory of
the One so near...

transform us now!
From teeth that gnash -
give us Your beauty
from the ash....   *Isaiah 61:3 NIV

of dusty roads and dying towns
of rivers dry,
where thirst abounds   *Matthew 5:6 NLT

where we hunger
for all, but Bread   *John 6:35 NIV
where our souls
are lost and often led

out into all that's vanity   *Ecclesiastes 1:2 NASB
depriving us of sanity...

as we stumble by night and day,   *Hosea 4:5 NIV
loosing sight of His Sweet Way.   *John 14:6 ESV

Oh, call us back from unseen danger!
Let us not answer to a stranger!   *John 10:5 ESV

As sheep before a Shepherd bleat
we cast our crowns now at Your feet.   *Revelation 4:10 ESV

So lend a smooth white stone
and a new name,   *Revelation 2:17 NASB
that we'll be no longer
sons of shame!

Iron Cast Heart

A dust boy—clothes stained and ripped,
a wrought iron treasure in his grip...

just some rusty scrape he'd hoped to mold
to watch its inner beauty unfold.

So he hobbled in from the cold winter,
as crutches would creak and splinter...

Under the weight of this boisterous child,
whose bent frame from offset by his smile.

But before speaking to ask his dad
if this old junk metal could be had,

he heard words that would forever sting,
"Oh! He's *crippled*! That poor little *thing*!"

"Crippled," he wondered, *"What does THAT mean?"*
Was it his legs? Was it the way that he leaned?

Despite good intentions that were had,
he just knew that it meant something BAD.

But he went about well on his way,
sorting through Dad's old scrapyard for play...

and taught himself how to do many things:
like welding bent nails into bowls for his King.   *Revelation 19:16 ESV

These bronze metal fruit bowls,
he would then turn
upside-down,
and weld on three crosses
for the One with the crown...   *Mark 15:17, John 19:2 NIV

to honor the Lamb,
more broken than he…
remembering Him
on old Calvary.

*1 Peter 1:19 NASB

A talent and patience this had required,
one that had been divinely acquired,

from his time spent bedridden in the past
and hours on end in full body casts.

But when the pain in his hip was too much
he'd pray for the LORD's invisible touch…

*Genesis 32:25 NIV

and it would come when the medicines had failed,
as strong and as sure as the bowls made of nails.

Then back good as new he would soon be,
up on his crutches and ready to flee…

and out to Dad's scrapyard fast like a fox,
this time to raid an old wrecker's glove box.

And a 1950's dictionary fell out on the seat,
so he blew off the dust to read in the heat.

*"Now what was that odd word
I was called on that day?"*
He wanted to see what
Mr. Webster would say…

"Crippled," he spotted on the
page with his finger,
and read it's meaning
as tears welled up to linger,

"A person or animal who is unworthy...unfit."
And he sobbed as this realization hit.

Despite all of his talents,
his mind, smile and cares—
all some people would see
were two crutches, wheelchairs.

An obedient child, no one
needed to scold him.
Never thought himself different...
until someone told him.

But that wasn't the only book he had read,
and defined himself by words written in red.

So the boy grew to be a man,
with faith and grace on which to stand...

He learned to draw and lived to love,
to be my dad—now gone, above.

And on his stone is etched a creed,
a lesson that we all should heed:
The Word to Samuel
is what sets God apart...
though man sees only flesh,
the LORD looks at the heart.   *1 Samuel 16:7 KJV

greed is a thorn
and pride is a thistle
but the trumpet's blast   *Revelation 11:15
will blow the whistle

on grave mistakes
and past offense,
to reconcile
and recompense

the chosen few
from all the nations
with angels faithful
at their stations

and a call to alms
through glorious psalms
that have been written
by servants, smitten

with One so GREAT
    and yet so *meek*   *Matthew 11:29
Who will be found
    by those who seek   *Matthew 7:7, Luke 11:9

One Flower for the Grave
For my father, Alvie Lee Whistler

I saw my father's grave today
no flower's
fragrant breath
could breathe new life
below the grass
and bring him
back from death.

I saw my father's grave today
no flowers
did I leave.
There are not enough fields of them
to match the loss I grieve.

I saw my father's grave today
no flowers
by my side,
and fake ones
cannot imitate
the love I feel inside.

I saw my father's grave today
before rushing out of town,
with the kniving agony
that I
had left him
in the ground.

What is it like beneath the earth
encased inside a box...
where back to ash and dust,
we fade into the rocks?

How can I leave him lying there
and simply

drive away—
as if he doesn't need my care
or someone just to stay…

and shelter him from all the cold,
the storms that winter sends?
And who'll be near
with hope to hear
his whispers in the wind?

What is my prayer
with him now gone?
What claim can my faith own?
I am not strong enough, myself,
to roll away the stone.   *John 11:39 NLT

But in the earth that covers him,
seeds feel on fertile ground—   *Matthew 13:8 NASB
with rain and light
to nurture them
until the spring abounds.

So I will watch his grave each year
with eager, steadfast urge…
to see what budding
Vine   *John 15:1 NIV
will come forth
and emerge!

Since I am known
by One Who says,
"…the dead will rise from tombs…"   *John 5:28-29 NLT
I only have to wait until
my sweet
Rose of Sharon   *Song of Solomon 2:1 ESV
blooms.

Shipwrecked

The storm is here
and closing in...
So oft' I ask -
was it my sin...

that caused the waves
to lap o'er head?
And winds to beat   *Matthew 7:25 NIV
so much I dread...

another breath, another day,
another time that I might stay—

confined within this cell to die
until I call on the Most High!   *Psalm 91:1 ESV

Who comes to me as gentle Brother,   *Hebrews 2:11-12 NIV
instills in me to love none other *Deuteronomy 6:5, Matthew 22:37 ESV

than Him first, the Triune Spirit;
that storms, He calms—no need to fear it!   *Mark 4:39 NASB

For every curse, He's there to break;   *Galatians 3:13 NASB
for every hurt, and each mistake...

He quiets the wind—says to be still,
and waves to cease all at His will.

I know my God, my refuge strong!
I cling to Him, 'mid every song...

and joyful noise that 'scapes my lips...   *Psalm 98:4 KJV
'spite stormy seas and desperate ships.

Turning Point

confined to die,
so tired and worn
with all my losses
that I mourn

a life so spent
and wasted time
I look back now
no reason, rhyme

the myriad of my mistakes,
the chances lost – the toll they take

where am I headed...?
which path to travel...?
as night creeps in,
as dreams unravel

into a lazy yesteryear,
fusing within a fallen tear

that trickles down my lonely cheek
where beauty's gone, where future's bleak

a memory is youth and hope
I cry inside, pretend to cope

what is a man or woman kind?
what purpose can we strive to find?

if all we are is ash and dust...   *Genesis 3:19 NASB
then who, are we, in whom to trust?

if this is all and nothing more,
who stands beside an open Door…?   *John 10:9 KJV

and does not enter, does not seek
a strength that's offered to the weak?

For all will fail, all will be lost
like ships under a tempest tossed

if we don't look across the waves
and reach out for the One Who Saves   *Acts 4:12 NASB

for in the darkness shines a Light   *John 8:12 KJV
an outstretched hand, a strength and might,

that raises us from certain death
that sparks to life sweet baby's breath

of a new soul who yearns for God,
a Sower's seed,   *Matthew 8:13 ESV
a Shepherd's rod   *Psalm 23:4 NASB

a narrow Way,   *Matthew 7:14
a still small voice   *1 Kings 19:12 KJV
that whispers we must make a choice

between this fate - so caustic, grim…
and one of joy with hope in Him   *John 15:11 ESV

Sweet Balm of Gilead

There is a Balm in Gilead,   *Jeremiah 8:22 KJV
Its fragrance sweet...
so it's been said.

There is a Balm in Gilead,
Its bark is dark...
Its flowers, *red*.

There is a Balm
coming at a price--   *1 Corinthians 6:19-20 NIV
our soul It takes
but saves our lives...

from the eternal second death,   *Revelation 20:14 NIV
what sorrows bring in Baby's breath...   *Matthew 24:8 KJV

that grip us, haunt us, night and day
as we toil, and pine, and pray –
but rest assured, He's made a Way   *John 14:6 NASB
for His impending Judgment Day!   *Revelation 20:13 NIV

There is a Balm in Gilead
as wand-like branches reach out to spread...

Good News about His safe return,
to one and all whose healing yearns...   *Revelation 22:2 NIV

for a great faith that makes them whole,
Yeshua plays a central role!

He is the Balm of Gilead,
make Him your treasure first instead...   *Luke 12:34 NIV

and feel the joy, the great relief
from all you suffer - even grief!

He is the Balm of Gilead—
Who calms the sea!   *Mark 4:39 NASB
Who wakes the dead!   *John 11:43-44 NIV

"Come!" He calls, as trumpets blast...   *1 Corinthians 15:52 NASB
as heavens burst open at last.

Come to the Balm of Gilead--
for tears that Jeremiah shed.

House Call

A little mess,
some here and there,
a pile of junk—debris;
At first
we do not notice it
'til we are
on our knees.

We ignore
the sight of it,
distractions
come and go
and we walk right through the filth
and it piles up and grows.

But soon before we know it,
disease has taken hold.
And we are ill,
for our own will,
has left us with a cold.

The virus hangs and feeds on us...
as it must run its course.
Make us shake and feverish
until the day we're forced...

to make a choice for life or death,
to rise or to succumb.
To face our fears
despite the tears,
knowing what we have become.

Accepting that in our own strength
there's never been a means,

to rid the grime
at any time
or hope to make us clean.

'Cept when we surrender
-let tumble down our walls-
for the Great Physician   *Matthew 9:12, Mark 2:17, Luke 5:31 -ESV
Who has come
to make a *call*.

What Grace is Like

God's grace is like
    a gentle wind   *John 3:8 NIV
    that soothes our wayward souls,
it cradles us
despite the fuss
    of all that's taken tolls.

God's grace is like
    an unbruised reed,
    a dimly burning wick—   *Isaiah 42:3 NASB
that's not snuffed out
despite our doubt
    and hearts that are so sick.   *Jeremiah 17:9 ESV

God's grace is like a *treasure*, found!   *Matthew 13:44 KJV
A living water river...   *John 4:14 NIV
    that flows to drench,
    our thirsts to quench   *Matthew 5:6 NASB
      as a tender lover's quiver.

God's grace is like a *precious* pearl   *Matthew 13:45-46 NKJV
of exquisite price—
    no matter the cost,
    to save the lost
while the cock crowed twice...   *Mark 14:72 NASB

for grace is love and truth, in one,
    a favor we cannot merit;
but only savor
without waver
    and answer a call...to share it.

To Those Who Love Me
(Exodus 20:6)

No white picket fence,
where all was fine...
I came from chaos
and fear, sublime.

I heard the screaming
vicious names;
I felt the rage –
adulterous games.

I knew no peace
or so I thought,
'cept through prayer
more things were wrought...

than I had dreamed of
from a little bed,
asking You, God,
Who once had said:

all things are possible
with You alone.   *Matthew 19:26 NASB
A child, I went boldly
to Your throne.   *Hebrews 4:16 KJV

And You calmed
the storm in me,
pursued me when
I tried to flee.

Convicted me when
I would need it,
called me to know
Your Word and heed it.

I grew to be a woman, still,
that knows Your voice and seeks your will.

I called to You, my Adonai,
begging for love from the Most High.

And I was given
a strong, true man-
who loved me back,
who took my hand...

and placed on it a golden band—
as time would tell, he would withstand...

the sling and arrows
of my whim
and love me still
when hope was slim.

This man restored
me to the full...
like a gentle king
who is sent to rule,

not with iron thumb or fist
with but a soft and tender kiss,

he led me out of desert halls,
he broke the chains of prison walls...

put life inside
and let it grow,
with pride and joy
that over flows...

so no more pain have I to nurse.
since God has broken every curse.   *Exodus 20:5-6 ESV

The Plants

Once a woman received
some large, flowery plants as gifts.
They were beautiful, and she
she was very proud   *Proverbs 16:18 KJV
of them.

But after time,
because of circumstances
that were beyond her control,
the plants got stuck
in a darkened   *John 3:19 ESV
corner of the patio.
Light did not reach them, then
old man winter
slithered in
and sat around,
its icy breath
in a silent coil
around the branches.

By the time she noticed
the plants again
in the springtime,
they were barely recognizable.
Their branches were cracked and gray.
They had no flowers, or even leaves—
much less, *fruit*.   *Galatians 5:22-23
And their warped, scaly limbs
stuck out like
crooked thorns.   *Matthew 13:7, Mark 4:7, Mark 8:7 NIV

But when she looked closer,
at the base of the plants—near the roots,
she saw that it was green! She thought,
"How can this be? How can

there be life
in something
so seemingly dead?"
Still, the plants were ugly.
They did not fit in
with her plans
for a new garden,
and she even considered
throwing
some of them
away.

Now, even though these plants
had been given to her
as a gift
as were not for her
to waste,
it was mainly for the sake of
the her own hopes
and her own dreams
of a new garden
that they were spared
for a time
from the fire.

So she put them in the Light...   *John 8:12
and let the rain fall on them.   *Deuteronomy 32:2 NASB
She didn't know what to expect,
or even what to hope for.
Whether or not
the plants would grow again
was beyond her control.
She could not
pry into
those branches,
with her
mere mortal hands,

and pull the sap
from the roots to the tips—
no matter
how much
she wanted them
to be *saved.*   *Titus 3:5 NIV

She just knew that plants
cannot refuse the Light.
They crave it.
They grow toward It
instinctively
for warmth and nourishment.

Can I tell you what
happened to her surprise?
After taking in the Light,
with the rain,
little green buds began to pop
out of gray, cracked branches!
It was a tiny miracle to see.
Now pure green-gold
is fusing through
those old, dry stalks.

And she *believes*
these plants
will bloom again.

The Light is our God, Yeshua.
   The woman is His bride.
      The plants are individual denominations.
   The branches are the congregations.

Keep lighting your Light shine, Pastors...
...and branches...
will bend.

When Lightning Comes

(Matthew 24:27)

When lightning cracks
it splits the black
    of night into small fractions.
It's aim lets us find
our sight from the blind
    and sparks a call to action.

Crisp volts from Heaven
pierced   *Isaiah 53:5 NASB, John 19:34 ESV
    seventy times seven,   *Matthew 18:22 KJV
    at last—it makes connection
with a true conduit
gentle and fluid,
    living water   *John 7:38 NIV
    will pose no rejection.

Then energy streaks
through seas and creeks
    as the body of water
        comes *alive*.   *1 Corinthians 15:22 NIV
And passing strangers
imagine a danger
    from being touched
        by the tide.

That water, thought weak,
though still supple and meek
    becomes a force beyond measure.
With no shape of its own
now it has grown
    to house the most powerful treasure.

But wood is so dense   *Deuteronomy 28:36
-tightly packed, takes offense-
   and offers the lightning
      no room…   *Luke 2:7 KJV
wood poses a barrier
and won't be a carrier
   for the only source
   to break the gloom.

And lightning will undo
what it can't
get through to—
   rough barks, bitter limbs are to blame.
So when lightning hits,
wood splinters a bit,
   before it ignites into flame.

That strong and dense wood
that once loomed and stood
   on it's on muddied ground and rich grass,
will fall
   in a crash
to be smothered in ash
   like remains from a house
      made of glass.

So true strength is deceptive
when we are receptive
   to the lightning's bright rapid pace,
in the comforting rod   *Psalm 23:4 KJV
that comes from You, God,
   in the form of Your swift, silent grace.   *Hebrews 4:16 NIV

The Laundromat *Mark 9:3 NIV

Last night
I dreamed that
I had run out
of clean clothes.

Then upon
stumbling   *Psalm 37:24 NIV
throughout the
darkened corners
of my closet
and under the
shadowy secrets
of my bed,
I finally found
my garments
scattered
all apart
in the dirt.

Having not a washer,
nor the time
for such a homey task
as hand-washing,
I was forced
to air my dirty laundry
before the public view.

So there I was.
I edged to the
local laundromat
and soon hurled
my ugly load
at the feet

of an old
washing machine.

Then I realized
that I'd forgot my wallet
and had nothing
in my
possession
to pay for the mess
that was
long since ground
into my clothing.

And I was all alone
in the empty room,
or so I thought.

That's when
a bent figure
appeared
from the corner
of my eyes.

His presence
startled me.
Ashamed,
I turned
to see Him.

What is He doing here?
I asked myself.
Just standing there...
what does He wait for?

That's when
my eyes caught His Own,

He had such bold eyes
that burned into my soul
and my heart sank.

Then He smiled
with lips parting
to say hello.

But questions hit me.
What was wrong?
Why had I waited
so long to wash my clothing?
Did He ask this
with His voice…
or through those
burning eyes   *Revelation 19:12 ESV
of His?

Had He asked at all?
Or had I asked myself?
I can't remember now.

But feeling pinned
to answer,
I offered an excuse
that just happened
to be true,

"I have no money
to pay for this load.
I left all
my belongings
behind today."

"Come,"
He said warmly,

"You can put them
in with Mine.
I also
left all My belongings
behind
and have little to spend,
but I will make
room for your own.
I don't mind
to pay for your load."

Flustered and confused,
but grateful—
I tossed my
filthy rags   *Isaiah 64:6
into His washer.

Had had only one robe,
pure white as wool.

Then I turned to this
new Friend   *John 15:15
with a remnant of
angst and guilt,
crying…

"HOW can I
EVER repay You?
You seem to have
so little, and yet
You still give.
And Your robe
is so clean and fresh…
as pure as the
Bright Morning Star!   *Revelation 22:16 NASB
But mine—so dirty!

Won't they stain Your robe?
I've just never been
able
to get rid of
those stains
by myself."

His Word--   *John 1:1-4 NIV
it was
warm and loving,
as I began to wake,

"Oh, Child,
can't you yet see?   *Matthew 13:16 NIV
Your DEBT
has already
BEEN PAID,   *Colossians 2:13-14 NASB
and
everything
comes clean
in My wash."   *1 John 1:7 NASB

Author's Note:
I wrote The Laundromat when I was around 13 or 14 years old, shortly
after Christ saved me. It was during my parent's divorce, when my father
had become a poor man. He and I would load up the pick up trucks every
Sunday, and head to the local laundromat to wash our clothes together.
At some point, the LORD pressed upon me to write about the redemptive
power of His time on the cross, about the salvation He offers to one and
all. What is important to note here, however, is that the salvation – the
cleansing, it wasn't "free." A price had to be paid. But it was HE who paid
it, in full, to redeem us. But that doesn't mean salvation now costs us
nothing. As you see in this poem, there was a struggle...a sorrow over our
condition, and a need for CHANGE. A change that comes only through
repentance, a very willful turning from the sin and filth we once called
home. And it wasn't "easy" to load that mess into a truck and drive it

somewhere. It wasn't always "entertaining" to have to wait, as we in our struggles and perils have to wait upon the LORD's deliverance at times. It wasn't fun to air my most private matters before a myriad of unknown eyes. But it was NECESSARY. And for it, I was cleansed to walk in the newness of life...eternally.

When Truth Offends

A thorn bush grew   *Judges 9:7-20 NIV
so we named it king.
It offered no shade
but songs, it could sing.

And that was enough
to sway us indeed,
like little mice
     dancing off
          through the weeds...   *Matthew 13:24-30 ESV

...and into a ditch   *Matthew 15:14 KJV
blind mice,
such as we
did stumble into   *Mark 9:42-48 NIV
an abyss   *Revelation 9 NIV
     and dead sea.

And all the king's horses
and all the king's men
could never save us
from all the king's sin.

But we'll defend
those thorns til the end,
as standards bend
when Truth   *John 14:6 NASB
offends.

That Still, Small Whisper

What drives me to this cave of mine...?   *1 Kings 19:9 NIV
This place to hide and wail...?
'Bout everything & nothing…
fear of chaos, fear I'll fail.   *1 Kings 19:10 NIV

Sometimes I fear   *Philippians 2:12 NASB
for my own soul.
I fear I'm nothing more…
than all that I have come from,
generations past, galore.   *1 Kings 19:4 ESV

Of little people
clinging
to what
little faith   *Matthew 17:20 ESV
they knew…
of little faith
or victory o're sin,
as nagging shrews.

In You, oh LORD…
am I not more than this?
For if I'm not,
then send me straight
into the deep abyss.   *Revelation 9 NIV

But now
an angel's touch   *1 Kings 19:5 ESV
comes to me in the night,
pointing me to Living Water   *John 4:10-14 NIV
and toward the Bread of Life.   *John 6:48-50 NASB

I come and drink,
am satisfied,   *Isaiah 55:1-2 NIV

and hungering no more—   *Matthew 5:6 NLT
am strengthened for a journey   *1 Kings 19:8 ESV
forty days and nights in store...   *Genesis 2:17, Deuteronomy 10:10 - NIV

before I seek   *Matthew 7:7, Luke 11:9 NIV
sweet refuge   *2 Samuel 22:3 NASB
in a whisper,   *1 Kings 19:12-18 ESV
like a Balm   *Jeremiah 8:22 NIV

after wind,
and quake,
and fire   *1 Kings 19:11-12 ESV
comes tearing through me,
then a Calm   *Mark 4:39 ESV
will come over all my senses
calling me
to live for Christ,
letting His sweet sword of truth   *Hebrews 4:12 NASB
cut through my soul just like a knife...

deep down into the marrow
of my spirit, mind, and heart—
dividing all that's in me
until
I AM   *Exodus 3:14, Mark 14:62 - NIV
set apart...

For this, His will, I'll walk into
the winds, earthquakes, and fire
to shake the souls asleep   *Ephesians 5:14 ESV
with a waking message DIRE...

that our God is
    an all consuming flame,   *Hebrews 12:29 NIV
burning the dross   *Malachi 3:3 NLT
in lives so lost
    who call upon His name.   *Romans 10:13 NIV

The Quickening

A tiny little flutter
stirs from deep inside
-*she questions*-
as it startles her,
and she does not know why...

at first,
where it has come from
just prompting there within-
jumps, abounds, and stops
so soon before it starts again.

This tiny bit of Life,   *John 14:6 NIV
it jolts
within the bride;   *Ephesians 5:25-33 ESV
she cannot sleep
with hunger deep   *Matthew 5:6 ESV
for Bread   *John 6:35 NIV
    & *meat*   *1 Corinthians 3:2 KJV
       & wine.   *Matthew 26:27-29 NIV

So it's not her own
-this *movement* now-
it comes while she
lay *still*;   *Psalm 46:10 ESV
comes as she pines and waits;   *Isaiah 40:31 ESV
and watches;   *Matthew 25:13 NIV
for it to beat at will.

And then she knows,
it's all so clear
-laughing-   *Genesis 18:12 NASB
she'll realize...
that Life has breathed   *Genesis 2:7 NIV

into her womb
and has called one to rise.

As cells divide
like ancient seas;   *Exodus 14:21-22 NIV
as Lazarus
was raised;   *John 11:43 NIV
as storms were silenced
on the spot
and all stood so amazed.   *Mark 4:35-41 ESV

Who has this voice,
authority-
calling life at His command?
Who stirs us from
a deadly rest
to ask
how
we can withstand…

this gentle nudge,
this fleeting twinge,
this stirring
from down deep...
this quest
to want Him more and more
that wakes us
    from our sleep.

It grows and grows
as time goes on,
as hunger
    drives her – craving...
like mad
for whatever she can find
to satiate the raving.

And much is offered up for her
in this her time of need
by well-intentioned
passers-by,
so on what will she feed?

Spend wages
for what does not satisfy   *Isaiah 55:2 NIV
as she whines and thirsts…?
Will she incline
her ear
to die,
and take advice
that's worse…

to pay for what
was never Bread…
to starve with
good news   *Luke 4:43 NIV
left unread.

What does she want…?
or does she covet…   *Exodus 20:17 NIV
a little god,   *Revelation 9:20 NIV
so she can love it?

One who won't demand too much,
but who will lend a healing touch.

One who stays out or her way,
and hasn't really much to say.

One that leaves her dead in sin
that she loves more, along with men.   *John 12:43 ESV

One who never challenges
her thoughts, and dreams – beliefs…
one who plays it safe,
and that she can neatly leave…

right in her back pocket,
where its comfortable & shady -
one who never stops her cold
or who sends someone to Hades.

A nice and tidy god
she wants,
one fit for all occasion-
one who won't *offend* too much
or won't compromise persuasion.

And yet the Father
waits in the wings
of this situation, dire—
for He knows exactly what
His Baby
will require…

EVERYTHING
-the bottom line-
right down to her marrow,
for her surrender
of own life   *Luke 17:33 ESV
just as a falling sparrow.   *Matthew 10:29 NIV

So she'll toss, but turn…   *Acts 3:19 NIV
while she does learn
    to be a proper host
of Life within
and then attend
to just what matters most:

hard labor
and her sacrifice,
with these she'll make the mark...
not by desire
of what the flesh aspires
in the world   *1 John 2:15 NIV
lukewarm,   *Revelation 3:16 NIV
and dark.

Until then this little movement
everyday it grows,
just like the pining question
Nicodemus came to pose...   *John 3:4 NASB

But who can hear it?
'Cept those born of the Spirit
        for it comes just like the wind...   *John 3:8 NASB
and we have no power
of the place or the hour
        when it will
                come again...

as a tiny little flutter
that stirs from deep inside,
not of our own
but from the Throne
calling for the soul to *rise!*

The Shroud Man

We rest
in a pasture
with clouds overhead.
They glide
in soft splendor
o'er the living and dead.

We watch
in quiet muse
the shapes they create,
shifting above us
in a gradual gait.

We try
　　to surmise
the whims of the skies,
as edges of clouds
　　　　drift and scrimmage.

And if we rely
　　on our mere mortal eyes,
　　　　we spot only an ash
　　　　　　graven image.   *Exodus 20:4 KJV

For our own perception
has suffered deception,
　　and left us unable to see
what has true form
apart from the norm
　　of all that we know and believe.

But should God let us spy
through lit beams of His eyes
　　a vision of gold is revealed—

from an old linen cloth
uneaten by moth
    comes a *Truth*   *John 14:6 NIV
        no tomb could conceal!

And His silver lining
dawns a star   *Revelation 22:16 ESV
    so refining...   *Malachi 3:3 ESV

...that its great gleam must
be sent to redeem us.   *Titus 2:14 NASB

So we'll wait   *Isaiah 40:31 ESV
in slow wonder
at the billowing thunder
    created by some sonic boom—
'neath a moon
red as wine
dark as blood, so divine,   *Revelation 6:12 ESV
fearing not   *1 Peter 3:14 NIV
    any damning or doom.

Escaped from Turin!
And coming again—   *Revelation 22:20 NIV
    to tear apart
    our imagined cloud man,
straight down from Heaven
comes *Sweet Manna*—unleavened   *John 6:32 NIV
    unfolding as...
    the "Shroud Man."

Years ago, I was intrigued by an article about the infamous Shroud of Turin, a piece of cloth that many people may believe to be the actual burial shroud of the Messiah—Yeshua, Jesus Christ. As a Christian, at first I was a little offended – because throughout the entire article, the author kept referring to the image merely as "Shroud Man." It struck me as being a bit irreverent...after all, He came to a lost world and redeemed the sins of all humanity to a Holy God, only to be called a "Shroud Man?"

But then it occurred to me that just as the Shroud of Turin itself is a mystery, the earthly life of our LORD was (and is) still a mystery to many.

And so, the imagery for this poem came to me gradually. I pictured children (like God's children everywhere) laying on a field discerning shapes in the distant clouds. And I recalled that Christ said He would come in the clouds.

So the ash graven image, our "imagined cloud man" in this poem represents our idolatry and worship of false prophets.

But our returning Christ, Yeshua...in this poem He is presented as the Sweet Manna (the Bread of Life) from Heaven, literally – the Bread of Life that was without "leaven," or sin.

And I would like to add that the authenticity of such a piece of cloth is largely irrelevant to my faith. That's because my faith in centered on the finished work of Christ on Calvary, His resurrection, and the tangible change this has brought about in my own life. But I think of the Shroud of Turin is a beautiful mystery, to be sure.

Twilight Time

darkness falls
descends on me

from time to time
with no relief

immediate, in my sight
as my soul cries out for Your Light   *John 8:12 NIV

I am alone in present grief
I am apart from my beliefs

the enemy has sought me out
& stolen from me, joy - as doubt   *John 10:10 NIV

like some cold fog surrounding me
my once sweet soul, abounding free

now broken by pain, so unrelenting
apart from You...no use repenting

or so it tempts me, leads me astray
to think the sun has lost its rays

to think the ocean has no waves
to think a prophet has no cave   *1 Kings 19:9 ESV

to hide oneself, take shelter there
for a small voice, still whisper where   *1 Kings 19:12 NIV

we are questioned to our core
of whereabouts and so much more...

where are we in our angst and pain?

where are we in our sin, abstained?
where are we in the desert heat?
where are we in our soul's defeat?

"Where are *you*, Child?" This Present Friend...   *John 15:15 KJV
seeks to know us more just when

we are so lost and so alone,
but calls us boldly 'fore His Throne!   *Hebrews 4:16 KJV

For He was tempted, tried but true   *Hebrews 4:15 NIV
& lives again to make us new   *2 Corinthians 5:17 NIV

come wind and earthquake,
fire and flood -
all mere precursors
to His blood...

that's spilled for each and every one
who turn from self and toward the Son

yes, in my sorrows, fear – unrest
there comes a Shepherd's call, request

"Come, follow Me and hear My voice..."   *John 10:27 NASB
beseeching me to make a choice

I welcome Him, my soul cries out
and I'm delivered from all doubt

how do we see?
how can we hear?

With His warm touch,
that's always near...
that opens eyes and

hearts and ears...

that cradles us in sweet relief,
restores our souls amid the grief

    of earthly life so frail and fleeting
    of failures past & sin competing

for our attention, time, and souls...
until the fateful church bell tolls...

    right up until that present hour
    when we submit to Higher Power

and see the Light   *John 8:12 NIV
to which we bend,
from desert heat...
this gentle Wind   *John 3:8 NIV

    will whisper still to us again
    our LORD & Master, God & Friend!

Three Trees

Tree of knowledge
tree of life…   *Genesis 2:9 NIV
forbidden fruit
that caused such strife.

Tempting woman,
testing man
& yet we ask
was this God's plan?

How could He let
such tragedies -
as famines, floods,
atrocities…

bear down on us infernally,
leaving some to die eternally?

To roast within the second death   *Revelation 20:14 ESV
the lake of fire that's satan's breath…

how can it be, this God is *just*?
But question Him, oh, if we must –

and find just what the prophets say
about the Potter and His clay: *Isaiah 64:8 NASB

How there came a Man of sorrows,   *Isaiah 53:3 ESV
same yesterday and tomorrow…   *Hebrews 13:8 NIV

Who walked among us in our grief
and felt it, too, with no relief…   *Hebrews 4:15 NASB

from torturous wounds by which we're healed -　　*Isaiah 53:5 ESV
this gospel truth has been revealed...

to hearts as humble as a child,　　　　　*Matthew 18:4 NASB
first to the Jew and then gentile:

He came despite the pain afflicted;
He came as all servants predicted;
He came beside the thief and more...　　*Luke 23:39-42 NASB
He came while sacred veils were tore.　　*Matthew 27:51 KJV

He comes again to old dry bones,　　　*Ezekiel 37:1-10 KJV
breathing new life straight from the Throne;
He comes to us for this and more,
bringing a balm – our soul's restore;
He comes though we welcome Him not,
purveying peace where we have fought;
He comes to burn away the dross,　　　　*Malachi 3:3 NLT
if we but take up our own cross...　　　　*Luke 14:27 NIV

And He will come to wipe our tears,　　*Revelation 21:4 NIV
renew our faith – assuage our fears;
And He will come to celebrate,
a wedding feast – an open Gate;　　　*Revelation 19:9 ESV
And He will come to reconcile
worlds that once, Him had reviled;　　*Romans 11:25-32 NIV
And He will come as trumpets call,　　*1 Corinthians 15:52 NLT
the quick and dead, as Judge of all!　　*2 Timothy 4:1 KJV

So when we suffer in despair
and Him might question, "Is he – where?"
Know this much with darkness nigh,
Who suffered *most* is the...Most High.

For on a third, dark blood-stained tree
He sealed our fates eternally...

Giving of grace that's so profound –
a pardon, pass, to holy ground...

one we can't steal, earn, buy, or sell!
What Eve had lost when Adam fell!

As filthy rags, our best works lie,   *Isaiah 64:6 NIV
our hearts are sick, our bodies die...   *Jeremiah 17:9 ESV

but still, He comes amid the rift
'tween LORD and man with hallowed Gift –

for in His place, there was no ram   *Genesis 22:13 NASB
to sacrifice, only the Lamb.   *1 Peter 1:19 NLT

How much is Love? What is the cost...?
to ransom we who are so lost...?   *Mark 10:45 NIV

And Who would give Himself and Child
to butchery and loathsome guile...?

'Cept One Who Saves and intercedes,
Who has felt all our wanton needs –

so qualified, this Advocate,   *1 John 2:1 NIV
our case, He pleads, from where He sits

by Adonai, at His right hand...   *Mark 16:19 NIV
as Son of God and Son of Man.

The Brink

Tossed at sea,
this rocky boat,
it cracks against the Wind...   *John 3:8 NIV
and waves do bear
but do not dare
pray for storms to rescind.

For I am lost
on maiden voyage
with weather less than fair...
and out of hope
when a noose's rope
brings comfort, not despair.

For at any time
I could end it,
and knowing that's control...
or so I think
I'd rather sink
than let fate take its toll

on what's left of sanity,
my body's aging state—
should I fear
an end is near
when all I've had, to date...

is misery
and heartache—
how much can a person take?
When grief looms
like some drizzly fog
round all my past mistakes.

I gasp for breath,
feel close to death,
and stumbling
    in my gait;
for this albatross
of pain and loss,
I smother neath its weight.

What have I done?
Was it too much? Or simply not enough?
Of everything
and nothing
that's seemed to call a serpent's bluff.

Am I a pawn
moved cross a lawn
of checkered celestial game?
And should I be
on bended knee,
or curse God and die—in shame?   *Job 2:9 NIV

So many questions
posed to me
and I cannot begin
to discern
-their answers, learn-
and choose not to pretend...

that I am more than dust and rib,   *Genesis 2:22 NIV
a worm despised by men,   *Psalm 22:6 NIV
a donkey given speech   *Numbers 22:21-33 NIV
that I might turn this path from sin.

And so no time for pity
and no time for wailing cries.

No time for anything
but finding blessings in disguise.

For from the dark
of a long ark
an olive Branch   *Isaiah 11:1 NIV
    did surrender...
its leaf to the Dove   *Genesis 8:11 NIV
of grace and love
sustaining hope so tender:

for a lost world's
New Covenant   *Matthew 26:28 NIV
that was bowed up in the sky,
raised up in all its glory—
like the One Who came to die.

And when I see
the faith in Hebrews,
of those who've gone before...
I question mine,
examine it,   *2nd Corinthians 13:5 NIV
knowing that I'll need much more.

But how can I attain it,
and where will it reside,
in a heart so dark
and jaded
like a stone that's cast aside?

So take all that is in me
when doubt creeps up in the night;
and dross, do purge
-let faith emerge-
and bless me in Your sight...

for I'm weak, as grains of sand,   *Hebrews 11:12 ESV
that beg of some great ocean
to be washed   *Revelation 1:5 KJV
despite the cost
and all of my emotion.

Now strike the colors
of my mast—
in here, this lonely vessel
and set apart   *Psalm 4:3 NIV
this wayward heart
with whom God, alone, might wrestle.   *Genesis 32:24 ESV

The Man Delusion

the **man** delusion
does not compute
it spins its wheels
in vile dispute

demanding evidence
pining for proof
it looks to beakers
instead of Truth

*John 14:6 NIV

ignoring One risen

*Mark 16:6 NIV

from the dead
ignoring, too,
the words in red

those, we'll avoid
at at each and every turn
for they ignite
Holy Fire, in return

we'll just pretend
that He never existed
and muddle through
with salvation resisted

and in the mean while
we'll try to buy
our worth in
plastic paradigms

the **man** delusion
is one that confounds
it runs it course
round and round:

poor in spirit, without hope
lacking proper Way to cope

mourning from its every loss
bitter, counting all the costs

meek enough to inherit earth
but never telling of its worth

a hunger that will not relent
rejecting all sweet nourishment

merciful to all its own,
but hateful to those unknown

pure enough in heart to try
but loosing sight of One so high

for making peace—we seldom care
except with sin, hate, and despair

longing to see some restitution
but fearing any persecution

instead, adore weak platitudes
that don't reflect beatitudes

keep seeking love that can't be found
in money spent or fame renowned

yet this **man** delusion
says there's no rod
to fall
from saying,
"There's no God."

Family Business

We all know the rules
of supply and demand.
Our economy is based
on such golden plans.

What's wanted most
will sell off the shelf.
It's just a matter
of catering to wealth.

Something so beautiful,
trendy and new,
will catch the attention
of mankind, that's true.

But I have a grand Father
Who deals in junk,
and He has
moved mountains   *Mark 11:23 NIV
of scrap metal gunk.

His business is an eye sore
to some who come near,
for their eyes cannot see
and their ears cannot hear...   *Jeremiah 5:21 NIV

...oh the sound
of my Father's
raging fierce flame!   *Exodus 3:2 KJV
White hot,
but contained,
like a paintbrush so tame.

He takes those old metals,
so twisted and warped,
and molds them as finely
as David played his harp.   *1 Samuel 16:23 KJV

Until they become
some new--
om His Own image.   *Genesis 1:27 NASB
Works of fine art,
with no wrinkle, spot, or blemish.   *Ephesians 5:27 KJV

And so,
me and Brother,   *Hebrews 2:11-12 NIV
we go out to find…
more pieces
for Father
to mold in His time.

And I don't really know
much about what to do,
because I am too little--
see, it's Big Brother Who…

…can spot the right pieces
on His judgment, I rely…
because it's well known
that He has Father's eye.

So He can tell
the good junk from bad,
what can be recycled
from what
WILL NOT
be had.

And so Brother guides me
through mounds of trash--
keeping me safe from
the rats, snakes, and ash…

…all for Our Father   *Matthew 6:9 ESV
-Who carries a torch-
for these pitiful pieces
in need of His scorch.

As He picks them up,
and blows the dust off--
matter will scatter,   *Ezekiel 22:15 NIV
while He wipes the must off.

He pulls down His mask
so we can't see His face,   *Exodus 33:20 NIV
but we see all the sparks
from behind   *Exodus 33:23 NIV
as His grace…   *John 1:16-17 KJV

…is revealed in the most unlikeliest place,
when beauty emerges from ash and disgrace.   *Isaiah 61:3 KJV

It's not for the money,
Father's wealthy enough--
but He'll make His prophets
call the enemy's bluff…

…as if he has a right
to take Father's place…   *Isaiah 14:12-14 KJV
steal, kill, and destroy   *John 10:10 NIV
in a futile mad race.

Even still, we'll watch Father's
wield more pieces together,

like a strong iron-cast quilt
to withstand the weather…

…some one hundred,
forty-four thousand   *Revelation 14:1 NIV
old odds and ends
will from an iron structure
soon just within…

…a matter of time
and through reasonable measures,
as mankind's old trash
turns to   *Ezekiel 18:30 NIV
the Son of Man's treasure.

Author's Note:
As a child, my paternal grandfather owned a scrape yard known as
"Whistler's Machinery & Supply" in Corsicana, TX. It was an EYE SORE.
Nothing but mountains of old metal and junk. But my father, a man
named, Alvie Lee Whistler, would find old pieces of metal to weld into
elaborate and beautiful sculptures. And my older brother, Michael Duane
Whistler, would help him. When our father suffered a terrible stroke, and
I moved home from Maryland to be with him for as long as I possibly
could…there were mounds of rusty scrape metal all over our father's
property. One day I asked my older brother why our father had moved
all this junk metal into his yard. Mike told me, "See…some of this is good
junk. It can be recycled, and Daddy knew which pieces to use for that."
Granted, we are told in Scripture that there is nothing innately "good"
about humanity. So there is is no "good junk" inside of us that can be
found, apart from Christ. For example, we are told that our best works are
like filthy rags before God. However, because it gave Him great pleasure
to redeem us…to salvage us…from the mess we created in Adam's fall, we
"turn to," meaning – we repent, to Christ. And God takes an old lump of
junk through the refining, baptismal fire of His Holy Spirit's conviction
and makes something *new.* Like the prophet Isaiah described, "Beauty
for ashes."

Words in Red

Someone said the words in red,
Someone said the words in red

now they've always been—   *John 1:1 ESV
and will always be,
but as far as
most mortal eyes can see:

before a word originates
whether it
      breeds love or hate
it must be whispered
thought or said
      and so it is with words in red

we cannot say, *they don't exist*
in all the pews—on book store lists

from hills to valleys, everywhere
the words in red make us aware

though opinions, we're entitled to
we can't deny one thing is true:

that Someone said the words in red
as many saw
His blood was shed
and Someone *said* the words in red

words seldom come out of thin air
words can't convict our sins out there

words, when used as a tool of man,
can't always dowse the flames they fan

words can disguise and can conceal
wounds only words in red can heal

for words in red have Life to give   *John 14:6 NIV
and they will forever live   *Matthew 24:35,Mark 13:31, Luke 21:33 NIV

our words may come and they may go
like kingdoms, cancers, fads, or snow

but keep this simple, so we know
how to avoid the undertow

for waves of words are rushing by
leaving some
        behind to die
and on those, we can't rely—
let words in red
        lift us
            up high…

to walk on waters deep with dread   *Matthew 14:29 NIV
to trample them neath heels instead   *Genesis 3:15 NIV

to die with them   *1 Peter 2:24 NIV
and bring to Life
His purpose, passion, plan, and wife

but in the mean time, we can tarry
spin our wheels until we're wary:

dispute if He was meek or vain
dispute if He was mad or sane
dispute if He was bred and born
dispute if He was sometimes torn
dispute if He resisted sin
dispute if He will come again

dispute if He was weak or strong
dispute if to Him, you belong

but we can't dispute The Gospel, read
for
it is written
and souls are led

duck or dodge them, here today
as prophets preach them, come what may

for JESUS
said those words in red
they have been published, pressed, and spread

passed the test, and fit to print
into all nations, they'll be sent

and you may doubt
or you may dread…
but
know you're LOVED   *John 3:16 NIV
by Whom they're said

Bird Man and the Dove

A Short Story dedicated to my late father, Alvie Lee Whistler

My father's hair was shaved, and fifty silver staples pierced the side of his head. His legs, deformed since childhood, accentuated his frailty. "A hemorrhagic stroke..." doctors recanted, "...spilled blood into the brain... the catheter will drain the excess fluid to stop the brain from swelling – any further..." Their silence was more comforting than their play-by-play commentary. And in that delicate moment the enemy spoke through a favorite form—someone with good intentions. "...maybe God gave your Daddy this stroke to get you to move back home."

I wasn't upset with the woman. She had no idea what possessed her to say that, just as I had no idea how to combat it. But that comment was the tip of the iceberg to my mountain of guilt. Years ago, my husband and I had moved away with the military, eventually settling on the east coast, far away from our childhood homes. Phone calls were the only way to bridge the distance with my dad. In our talks I could hear the happy chatter of Dad's parakeets. They offered motion and sound in his small home. My brother and his family were always there for our dad, inviting him to ball games and holidays. But I wasn't. And these chattering, tiny creatures were a subtle reminder that my father relied on birds, instead of my children, for his daily joy and companionship.

Watching his chest heave in time with the breathing machine, I decided not return to Maryland. Many obstacles stood in the way—our deep financial debt, our mortgage, our new pregnancy, and my husband's urgent warning that the economy wasn't stable in my home town. But I wouldn't listen. I wanted to stay with my father, so he wouldn't have to live in a nursing home. Everyone assumed his Medicare and Medicaid would cover the cost of in-home nurses. We could rent our house in Maryland state, and work opposite shifts in odd jobs until a better job came along in Dallas. But I could be there. It could work. Such was my hope.

Though seemingly unconscious, my father would respond to certain commands, like squeezing our hands when asked. But he suddenly he stopped responding to anyone or anything. The hospital staff never volunteered the word "coma" to describe his condition, until pinned for a direct answer. He had a feeding tube, a tracheotomy, and a catheter. Under the stipulations of his Medicare and Medicaid, he couldn't return home until he was "...down to only one tube." So at the time of his discharge, a nursing home was our only choice—for the short run, I had hoped.

Gradually, he began to come around. But he was now paralyzed on his entire left side. For the remainder of his life, he would be confined to a bed and wheelchair, completely dependent on others to survive. As a child, a bone disease destroyed my father's hip joint, causing a permanent disability. But he learned how to use crutches, and nothing could stop him. He cleaned house for his mother, and ran races in school. He would even mediate squabbles between his siblings—one stout toss of a crutch in their direction would settle most disputes. He'd been a draftsman, and had a fascination with turning old pieces of scrap iron into beautiful sculptures. He'd drop his crutches, scale a ladder, light his torch, and start to weld. At those times, I witnessed my father bending iron by his sheer force of will. So it was unthinkable, that such a fiercely independent soul would have to be bound now by bed sheets and circumstance. We met him with smiles in the desperate hope that if we seemed happy, he might not feel so bad. The arm that had once melted iron would tremble from under the blankets, like the helpless flutter of some wild creature —now caged.

And we soon faced another horrible truth. More often than not, he didn't recognize us, and was seldom aware of his true surroundings. His wry grin and twinkling eyes had been replaced by an expressionless, haunting stare. He would ask for his crutches repeatedly, forgetting that he was paralyzed. He would ask for food he could not eat and water he could not drink. On all three counts, we were told to deny him.

Perhaps what disturbed me the most was when he would also ask about deceased relatives, as if they were still with us. His questions always centered around the prospect of going to see them. For some mysterious reason, he was under the impression that they were accessible to him now. And I wondered if perhaps they had been for a time, given his recent experiences. They were foremost on his mind, moreso than us.

Missing my father had always been hard while living states away, but it was harder still to miss him while holding his hand. Often I would leave the parking lot of the nursing home screaming obscenities, and smashing my fists into the dashboard.

Much like Jacob, my father had spent a life time of *wrestling* with God. So many unhealthy dreams and aspirations often plagued his walk with Christ, ultimately bringing him to a place of destitution and isolation. One by one, the Almighty had hand plucked each and every little idol in my father's life away, quite simply and systematically...because ultimately, I believe, he belonged to God. And the last of these obsessions, was with alcohol.

When I was a child, my father used to tell the story of the little lamb held by Jesus in a famous portrait. In my father's tale, the little lamb would often stray. And so, to keep the little lamb from straying into a pack of wolves or over a cliff to its own peril, the Good Shepherd would hobble this particular wayward lamb.

"The Shepherd would take his rod, and he would break that lamb's legs," my father would explain to me. "But after the Shepherd broke its leg, the Shepherd would then carry the little lamb and raise him up. He would love the lamb and take care of it. And after a time, that little lamb would learn that all he ever really needed came from the Shepherd anyway. And the lamb would no longer stray."

Stripped, like Job, of everything by his late sixties, my father had only his drink left. And I wondered if the LORD had allowed this stroke in order to put my father in a position where he could no longer sin with excessive alcohol, thus removing the very last idol from his life.

But what ever the divine rhyme or reason to this horrific situation, soon other worries surfaced. Our house hadn't rented soon enough, and we faced foreclosure. The only available jobs did not keep us off food stamps or out of bankruptcy. Now four months pregnant, I contacted viral pneumonia. Then medical tests indicated that our new baby might have Downs Syndrome. That news came as quite a blow, since one of our children is severely affected by Autism. Could we manage another disability? And every time I visited my father, he would look me right in my eyes and ask, "Where's Leanne?" I would fight back a tear, gently pat his leg that still had feeling, and tell him hoarsely, "I'm Leanne, Dad. I'm right here."

In those darkest hours, the enemy would ask me where my God was. After all, I had "honored my father..." and had "taken a leap of faith..." so, where was He? After a while, the argument became convincing. So I screamed aloud at God one day. I told Him, quite frankly, that if all of this was part of His plan, then in my opinion His 'plan' SUCKED.

The still small whisper we know to be the Holy Spirit made me consider Christ and His suffering on the cross – a notion that I interrupted by yelling, "And why did JESUS have to go through all of THAT?! Why is there such misery?! YOU TELL ME WHY!!!"

But as is the case with any gentle-natured dove, too much ranting noise had made Him flutter smooth-cool AWAY. And there I was, left in the absence of God: a blank abyss with no meaning, reason, or hope. Life was just a time-killer. I cried face down, stinging tears into the carpet. I considered a life without God. What would it be like to gaze into the sunlit edges of a cloud and feel only the dreaded heat of another summer day? What would it be like not to feel His eminence and humble glory in the face of the sky? I could not imagine it. Even though I was still angry and confused, I resolved that I could not live without Him because of all His attributes—He is hope.

Then in my silence, gentle notions came to me. Faith is more than a belief—it is the very way through which we communicate with Christ. And without that, how can we expect Him to respond? That's like hanging up the phone on a trusted Friend then getting angry because He's not listening or answering our questions. Next I remembered the doctors explanations, "Frequent smoking and excessive alcohol can bring on a stroke." This suggestion was part of the doctor's sideline commentary that had been "less-comforting" for me to hear at the time. So for decades my dad had laid the groundwork for this situation. The stroke was not a *punishment* for sinning with alcohol, but was rather the simple physical consequence of prolonged unhealthy habits that God was now using to set my father apart.

And had *God* asked me to take my leap of faith, or had I been trying to enact my own will, assuming that it was His? Is it fair to jump off a cliff, and blame God when we hit the ground? These little revelations replaced my tears, coming not as criticisms, but as comfort. How amazing is such grace?

Three days later, my brother's church gave us a baby shower. A congregation who'd never met us donated endless baby supplies and a mountain of groceries. Family and friends brought gifts. And my aunt suddenly gave us several thousand dollars, just because she knew we'd been out of work. These acts of kindness converged in one weekend, after my decision to keep trusting God. Even during my doubts, He was prompting people to help us. And blessings continued. My husband found work. And a more promising job was later offered in another part of the state.

That posed a painful decision—staying in town meant staying on food stamps, perhaps indefinitely. Welfare had been a temporary means to an end, but we couldn't let it become a legacy for our children. Many obstacles hindered our move back to Texas, like road blocks I chose to ignore. But now circumstances fell right in line. It was like a way had been made through effortless forces, and we were compelled to follow.

Over the next year, we made regular trips to see my dad. During this time, he had recurrent episodes of pneumonia. In late August of 2006, his heart rate failed during CPR in his final bout with that disease. I was not there when he died. In spite of our efforts over the last three years, I had failed him one last time.

The funeral home was flooded with all of my father's old acquaintances. His housekeepers also came to see him, telling me, "Oh, we had to come see the Bird Man! That's what we called him! You know your daddy loved his birds!" Another man commented, "That old Alvie had more lives than a cat!" Their presence was yet another blessing. Their jovial nature and bright smiles reminded me that God's joy was still alive, and therefore, could return to us again someday.

And that same joy was with the pastor at the funeral. He was not sad, nor was he solemn. Instead, he had a smile a mile wide. His eyes were on fire with the brightest light, and he would give the devil no room. He told us,

"...I lived in a lot of houses. Some were shabby, and some were nice—but I've never lived in a house that is completely made of gold. Alvie Whistler has, though. He's been there since Tuesday." And that's when I realized that my dad now sees everything. He sees my efforts— that I had, for once, put him first—for as long as I possibly could have.

Days later, my sister-in-law had a dream. It is common knowledge in our family, that her dreams are prophetic in nature. This time she saw our dad walking, completely upright, as tall as any other man. He was content, unaware of anyone and unconcerned about anything—with no crutches, tubes, traches, or staples. As an eagle mounts up on wings to soar, our father now walks in a new found freedom...that has been granted...by the *grace* of a Dove.

I stood there in the pews, head bowed – not in prayer, but in anguish. I was standing, pensively, in a small little southern Baptist church with a new young preacher, who was on fire for the Gospel, and laying out his alter call.

But I wouldn't budge. Stubborn little prideful mule I was at the age of 14 or so. Yes – there were many things that pride would not permit.

Besides all of which, the anger over my parent's dissolving marriage had settled into me like some sort of alien sickness. And despite their lip service to Jesus, I could scarcely recall a time when I had been taken to any church as a small child. Of course our lovely home was cluttered with little religious plaques and symbols, along with the occasional and woefully ignorant, unbiblical *opinions* that my parents had tossed around about the Christ in front of me, and when such an atmosphere is also coupled with fury, profanities, pornography, substance abuse and a near total lack of love for one another...well, it can make a child quite jaded about the existence and involvement of any god – much less, the only real One.

And so, there I was – standing, solumnly, in the pews. *Why?* I asked unconsciously with every refusal to move, *why were my parents suffering – why was I?* Sure my grandmother had once sat me on her knee, telling me stories of how this Messiah had turned the water into wine, how He had raised the dead, and how He had died Himself for the sins of all the world. So if He was so amazingly capable, why was there such misery, not just in my own little life, but in the whole world at large? Frankly, in my estimation at the time, if He existed at all then He must be quite the divine Jerk for allowing it.

No, it wasn't so much that I didn't believe in God, as it was the fact that I was *mad at Him*.

Then breaking into my wall of resistance, the pastor added suddenly... but softly, "I feel the person whom the LORD is calling today *is* a youth."

My heart quickened.

Really, Padre? I remember thinking, *Well then – male or female? You'll have to be more specific than that if you expect ME to humiliate myself!*

Clearly, I wasn't into parlor tricks and psycho babble. This gentleman was going to have to do better than that if he expected me to embarrass myself in front of all these people.

Eventually, they closed the service. And a myriad of mixed emotions hit me. At first I was relieved. After all, I was off the hook now. But soon that relief caved into a sinking feeling that I had forsaken something, or Someone, far greater than I could ever imagine; Someone I didn't even know or understand...at least, not yet.

Next week, God. I bargained with the Almighty. *I'll go down during next week's alter call.*

But that is when I learned something about this Yahweh. And that is that He would not be "put off."

As I waited on the porch steps of the church for my brother and new sister-in-law to get their vehicle, I heard my name being called. I turned and – to my horror – it was the pastor himself. I dreaded any interaction with him. I suddenly felt like some undesirable vagrant who was caught trespassing on a rich man's property, like I didn't belong – or so I was led to believe, momentarily. Fearing reproach and certain judgment, I somehow summoned the courage to look this man in the eye.

And that's when I was quite surprised. His eyes were not cold and distant or disapproving – but bright and loving. He did not sneer at me for being such a lowly sinner, but smiled such a welcoming smile that I was captivated, drunk in the love that seem to exude from him so effortlessly. Whatever was flowing out of this man who grinned affectionately at me, all I knew at the time was that I flatly didn't deserve it.

And yet there it was: Grace. Mercy. Love.

He said, "Leanne...I felt like *you* were the person the Lord was calling today. And I just felt that He wanted me to give you this."

It was the New Testament.

I don't even remember what, if anything, I said in response. My jaw had dropped, spiritually. *Male or female..?* I had challenged this man. Umm...yea.

One thing was for certain. This guy didn't play. I wasn't invited to "Popcorn and Movie Night" for months and years on end in the vain hope that some of this "Christianity stuff" would rub off on me. I was not "entertained." And I reasoned, that if this man had the gumption to hit me sidelong with the truth like that, the least I could do was read what he gave me.

And that I did. I don't remember how many of the four Gospels I had read before the Spirit of our Holy God made me understand that He is not cold and distant and condemning, but that His mercies are new everyday. That once we come to Christ when we are called, our sin is blotted out and we are given a clean slate. That this Yeshua, this Jesus, is the Living Embodiment of Yahweh...in all His hard truth, yet amazing grace.

Do you know Him today? If not, then I say FIND. SEEK. Knock, and His door will be opened with so much grace that you will drown in it. You will die, yes, you but you will also come...to *life*.

Printed in the United States
By Bookmasters